Lin Yutang
THE BEST
OF AN OLD FRIEND

林語堂精摘

Lin Yutang

THE BEST
OF AN OLD FRIEND

Edited by A. J. Anderson
Foreword by Lin Yutang

MASON / CHARTER

NEW YORK 1975

FOR VICTORIA
THADDEUS
DERRICK

818.5
L

Library of Congress Cataloging in Publication Data
Lin, Yutang, 1895-
  Lin Yutang : the best of an old friend.

  1. Lin, Yutang, 1895-   --Quotations.
PR9470.9.L5A16 1975   808   75-34925
ISBN 0-88405-114-5

CONTENTS

FOREWORD

I am very honored that Professor A. J. Anderson, after spending laborious years of love, has gotten together from all my books certain lines said by me that seem quotable. And I am particularly glad that he calls these lines "the best of an old friend." In going over the manuscript, it was a continuous delight on my part to find so much that had Professor Anderson's approval. These were nothing but ordinary sayings "of an old friend" who could lay bare his innermost thinkings and had nothing to hide—before God or his mother.

I like an old Chinese writer who said: "The ancient people were not compelled to say anything, but they suddenly said something purely of their own accord. They spoke sometimes of events, and sometimes of their feelings, and having finished what they had to say, they took their leave and departed." And so, having written purely of my own accord, and having finished what I had to say, I take my leave and depart.

Lin Yutang

May 19, 1975
Hong Kong

ACKNOWLEDGMENTS

卅卝

The publisher and editor acknowledge with appreciation the permissions granted by the following copyright holders of Lin Yutang material for the reprinted excerpts used in this book.

Asia
"First Impressions in America: Letter to a Chinese Friend," *Asia,* November, 1936, pp. 744, 745.
"Chinese Humor," *Asia,* October, 1946, pp. 453, 455.

The Atlantic Monthly Company
"When East Meets West," *The Atlantic Monthly,* December, 1942, pp. 45–46.

Thomas Y. Crowell, Inc.
From Pagan to Christian. Cleveland: The World Publishing Company, 1959. Copyright © 1958 by Lin Yutang. Reprinted by permission.
The Importance of Understanding. Cleveland: The World Publishing Company, 1960. Copyright © 1960 by Lin Yutang. Reprinted by permission.
The Pleasures of a Nonconformist. Cleveland: The World Publishing Company, 1962. Copyright © 1962 by Lin Yutang. Reprinted by permission.

York Times Company. Reprinted by permission.
"The Real Threat: Not Bombs, But Ideas," *The New York Times Magazine*, November 12, 1939, pp. 1–2, 16. © 1939 by the New York Times Company. Reprinted by permission.

Random House, Inc.
The Wisdom of Confucius, edited and translated by Lin Yutang. Copyright 1938 and renewed 1966 by Random House, Inc. Reprinted by permission of the publisher.
The Wisdom of Laotse, edited and translated by Lin Yutang. Copyright 1948 by Random House, Inc. Reprinted by permission of the publisher.

Simon and Schuster and Clifton Fadiman
"I Believe" in *I Believe: The Personal Philosophies of Certain Eminent Men and Women of Our Time*, edited by Clifton Fadiman. New York: Simon and Schuster, 1939.

The University of Chicago Press
A History of the Press and Public Opinion in China. Chicago: The University of Chicago Press, 1936. Reprinted by permission of the publisher. All Rights Reserved.

INTRODUCTION

There are times in our lives when we need a friend to turn to—someone who will help us interpret life, who will put things into perspective for us, and from whom we can draw nourishment for living.

Lin Yutang is a friend for those times. After having been exposed to the shrill and unhappy voices of so many despairing people in recent years, to return suddenly to the quieter and more thoughtful voice of an old friend who has been standing by patiently, waiting to be called upon if needed, is quite an exhilarating experience. Let us ask him to speak again, for there are few thinkers more needed in the world today than this wise and calm observer of human life.

This book represents the essence of Lin Yutang's thoughts on almost every kind of topic under the sun. Here, within the compass of a single volume, are the discoveries he has gleaned from the experience of living. Here is what is good and what is bad in life, what is true and what is false, what to love and what to hate. No topic is too momentous or too insignificant for his pen, and he writes with equal grace and wit upon every kind of human emotion and experience—from tea drinking and lying in bed to democracy and juvenile delinquency. "I do not know whether I am more in dead earnest about light topics or in a lighter mood when dealing with serious ones," he states with characteristic candor. "I have no sense of their relative impor-

1

tance." But one has only to spend a few minutes in his company to realize that one has come in touch with a mind that is guided by reason, integrity, and sense of beauty.

Lin Yutang's family name is Lin, but he smiles understandingly when people refer to him as Mr. Yutang. He was born in Amoy, Fukien Province, on the southeast coast of China, in 1895, the son of a Chinese Presbyterian minister. He himself was destined for the ministry, but during his first months at St. John's University in Shanghai, whither he had gone after graduating from the Changchow Middle School, he lost interest in theological studies and became instead what he calls "happily a pagan." "I took to English like a duck to water," he says, and after receiving his bachelor's degree in 1916, became a professor of English at Tsinghua University in Peking, where he stayed until 1919. In that year, with his wife, Tsuifeng Lin (who is coauthor, with one of their daughters, of Chinese cookbooks), he journeyed to Harvard University to work on his master's degree—which he received *in absentia* in 1922. From Massachusetts the Lins traveled to France, where Dr. Lin found a job in the Paris YMCA teaching Chinese laborers who had been sent to France during the First World War. Shortly afterward he and his wife moved to Germany, where Dr. Lin studied at the University of Jena and Leipzig, earning his Ph.D. in 1923. His thesis dealt with old Chinese phonetics.

On their return to China that same year, Dr. Lin started teaching in the department of English at Peking University. In 1926, however, he and other liberal professors were blacklisted and eventually chased out of Peking by the "Dog-meat General." From Peking he traveled back to Amoy, to become Dean of Arts at Amoy University. With the rebellion then stirring in China, he had his first real brush with politics—and his last. He became Secretary in the Ministry of Foreign Affairs in the Wuhan Nationalist Government, but gave up the position when he realized that he was "a herbivorous, rather than a carnivorous animal,

2

vastly better at minding my own business than that of others."
He says of the experience, "When I got tired of that and saw
through the farce of revolution, I graduated into an author, partly
by inclination, partly by necessity."

Now launched on a writing career, he became a leader in a
movement to adapt Western newspaper methods to Chinese
journalism, and he founded and edited three literary fortnightlies.
In 1935 he also became associated with *T'ien Hsia Monthly*, an
English-language publication put out by the Sun Yatsen Institute
for the Advancement of Culture and Learning; the journal was
forced to cease operation with the advent of the Sino-Japanese
war. Many of the essays he wrote during these years appeared in
The China Critic, an English weekly of Chinese opinion published in Shanghai; several of these pieces are collected in two
volumes entitled *The Little Critic: Essays, Satires and Sketches on
China*.

With the publication of *My Country and My People* in
1935, Dr. Lin became known as an interpreter of the spirit and
mind of China to the West. The book was an immediate success,
and was subsequently translated into several languages—as most
of his writings have been. A year later the Lin family arrived in
the United States to take up residence in New York City. In 1937
Dr. Lin's most famous book—*The Importance of Living*—appeared, establishing him in Western eyes as one of the best known
and most original Oriental thinkers of all time. In this animated
synthesis of wisdom and humor, Dr. Lin expounds a philosophy
for living. He declares unabashedly that the purpose of life is to
enjoy it and has the courage to say that he is pleased with an
extraordinary number of things. He comes down hard on insen-
sitivity, inhumanity, complexity, and dogmatism; but at the same
time he is tolerant of human imperfections and understands the
folly that men do. He seeks not a perfect world, where nothing
surprising or untoward happens, but one in which the "Spirit of
Reasonableness" prevails.

3

Not a person to beat a timid retreat from the problems of life, he has spoken out courageously and with great passion when he felt the occasion called for it—as in his books *Between Tears and Laughter* and *The Vigil of a Nation* and in numerous periodical articles and letters to editors during World War II. Dr. Lin is also well-known for his translations of classic Oriental literature —*The Wisdom of China and India, The Wisdom of Confucius, The Wisdom of Laotse*—and he has written many novels, plays, travel books, and other monographs in English, producing a bestseller almost every other year. (A complete bibliography of Lin Yutang's English writings, prepared by this editor, appears in the April–June 1973 issue of *The Bulletin of Bibliography and Magazine Notes*.)

In 1948 Dr. Lin became Head of the Arts and Letters Division of UNESCO, and in 1954 he was chosen to be Chancellor of the new Nanyang (South Seas) University in Singapore. On that occasion the *New York Times* commented in an editorial: "We shall be sorry to lose from the American scene a witty and wise writer, speaker and philosopher. He has, happily, been with us so long that we count him almost as one of our very own." In April 1955, however, after a clash with the Communists, who wanted to establish policy at the university, he resigned. He and his family returned to the United States. After having renounced Christianity as a young man, he returned to the Christian church in 1957; his account of his odyssey from Christianity to paganism and back is to be found in his book *From Pagan to Christian*. He has recently completed *A Chinese-English Dictionary of Modern Usage*, a monumental work two decades in preparation—and the first by a Chinese scholar.

Pearl Buck, who first introduced Lin Yutang to the Western world, has given this account of him: "Anyone can talk with him with complete frankness and intellectual honesty, for his is an honest intelligence. He is afraid of nothing and no one. . . . He is sophisticated and keen and knows himself. He enjoys success

4

but he laughs at it and at himself a little, being at heart too large for petty vanity. He takes the truth without flinching and has an unshakable integrity of judgment beneath the brilliance of his talk. To a crowd which he feels is responsive he will deliver an entertainment of wit and laughter and hard hits. But if he doesn't like the crowd, he disappears into a slight, stiff, masked figure, academic and remote—and knows what he is doing and doesn't care." His English has been described by one reviewer of his writings as "certainly the very best any Chinese has ever written," and by another as "the style of a sophisticated contribution to *The New Yorker.*"

The selections in this book are assembled under twelve topic headings; but since, as Lin Yutang observes, "order is seldom exciting," no attempt has been made to arrange them in any particular order within the categories. Thus the book has neither beginning nor end. The best way to read it is to open it anywhere —and read. In a while the author's twinkling-eyed humor, his unfailing reasonableness, his wistful evocations, his natural relish for the simple and sensual pleasures of life . . . but let Lin Yutang speak for himself!

School of Library Science, A. J. ANDERSON
Simmons College,
Boston, Massachusetts

I CAN WRITE ONLY OF MY OWN PERCEP-
TIONS AND INSIGHTS AND MY OWN EVALUA-
TIONS AND INTERPRETATIONS.

—*LIN YUTANG*

人生幸福
及享受

1

ON HAPPINESS
AND THE
ENJOYMENT OF LIVING

☷

Oh, the sensuous delight, the pleasurable laziness of sleeping late, with nothing on one's mind, and the enjoyment of a perfect sleep!

Looking Beyond, p. 173

I am quite sure that amidst the hustle and bustle of American life, there is a great deal of wistfulness, of the divine desire to lie on a plot of grass under tall beautiful trees of an idle afternoon and *just do nothing*.

The Importance of Living, p. 2

The three great American vices seem to be efficiency, punctuality and the desire for achievement and success. They are the things that make the Americans so unhappy and so nervous. They steal from them their inalienable right of loafing and cheat them of many a good, idle and beautiful afternoon. One must start out with a belief that there are no catastrophes in this world, and that besides the noble art of getting things done, there is a nobler art of leaving things undone. On the whole, if one answers letters promptly, the result is about as good or as bad as if he had never answered them at all. After all, nothing happens, and while one may have missed a few good appointments, one may have also

11

avoided a few unpleasant ones. Most of the letters are not worth answering, if you keep them in your drawer for three months; reading them three months afterwards, one might realize how utterly futile and what a waste of time it would have been to answer them all. Writing letters really can become a vice. It turns our writers into fine promotion salesmen and our college professors into good efficient business executives. In this sense, I can understand Thoreau's contempt for the American who always goes to the post office.

The Importance of Living, p. 162

No one, I believe, can live in close touch with nature and its seasons, its snows and rains, its hills and dales, receiving its healing powers, and have a warped mind or a warped view of life.

The Gay Genius, p. 165

If a man will be sensible and one fine morning, when he is lying in bed, count at the tips of his fingers how many things in this life truly give him enjoyment, invariably he will find food is the first one.

The Importance of Living, p. 248

So much unhappiness, it seems to me, is due to nerves, and bad nerves are the result of having nothing to do, or doing a thing badly, unsuccessfully, or incompetently. Of all the unhappy people in the world, the unhappiest are those who have not found something they want to do. The proportion of people who go to mental hospitals is the measure of people who worry and do not work, not of people who work and do not worry. Nobody dies of hard successful work; one dies only of unmanageable work, purposeless work, work of a nature that drowns a man's nerves as the

12

sea drowns a man's body. This is a dangerous thing to say in America; too many die of heart attacks, of over-strain of their nervous system. But the truth is not known. One can die of hard work in the sense that one can die of over-eating, or even of walking, as in a Marathon race. But this is unfair to the idea of the normal function of working, eating or walking. Americans don't die of hard work, as I understand the sense of the word; they die, so many of them, of running a Marathon race with their nervous systems to see who is going to outlast whom. The ordinary laws of our animal being are not to be defied. But, short of defying common sense, true happiness comes to him who does his work well, followed by a relaxing and refreshing period of rest. True happiness comes from the right amount of work for the day.

On the Wisdom of America, pp. 222–223

After a sound sleep and a cup of fragrant coffee, a man is ready to conquer the world, optimistic, cheerful, vibrant, ready to tackle any problem that comes along.

The Pleasures of a Nonconformist, p. 117

O wise humanity, terribly wise humanity! Of thee I sing. How inscrutable is the civilization where men toil and work and worry their hair gray to get a living and forget to play!

The Importance of Living, p. 148

Poor Byron, who had only three happy hours in his life! He was either of a morbid and enormously unbalanced spirit, or else he was affecting merely the fashionable *Weltschmerz* of his decade.

The Importance of Living, p. 136

13

On the whole, the enjoyment of leisure is something which decidedly costs less than the enjoyment of luxury. All it requires is an artistic temperament which is bent on seeking a perfectly useless afternoon spent in a perfectly useless manner. The idle life really costs so very little, as Thoreau took the trouble to point out in *Walden*.

The Importance of Living, p. 153

I have no room for the professional pessimists, misanthropes, misogynists, "realists," and all those people who wish they had not been born upon this earth, but somewhere else.

On the Wisdom of America, p. 445

There is so much to love and to admire in this life that it is an act of ingratitude not to be happy and content in this existence.

The Pleasures of a Nonconformist, p. 51

I think sometimes the universe is not big enough to hold the heart of a child.

From Pagan to Christian, pp. 24–25

. . . inner calm is possible only when man is not disturbed by the vicissitudes of fortune.

The Importance of Living, p. 160

No one can be convincing when he is unhappy himself.

The Pleasures of a Nonconformist, p. 117

I think I know what I want. Here are the things that would make me happy. I shall not want other things.

I want a room of my own, where I can work. A room that is neither particularly clean nor orderly. No Mademoiselle Agathe of the "Story of San Michele" to dust everything she can reach with her dust-cloth. But a room comfortable and intimate and familiar. Over my couch hangs a Buddhist oil-lantern, the kind you see before Buddhist or Catholic altars. An atmosphere full of smoke and the smell of books and unaccountable odors. On the shelf overlying the couch are books, a good variety of them, but not too many—only those I can read or have read with profit again, against the opinion of all the book reviewers of the world. None that takes too long to read, none that has a sustained argument and none that has too much cold splendor of logic. They are books that I frankly and sincerely like. I would read Rabelais along with "Mutt and Jeff" and Don Quixote with "Bringing up Father." One or two Booth Tarkington, some cheap third-rate penny novels, some detective stories. None of those sentimental self-delineators for me. No James Joyce and no T. S. Eliot. My reason for not reading Karl Marx or Emmanuel Kant is very simple: I can never get beyond the third page.

I want some decent gentlemen's clothing that I have worn for some time and a pair of old shoes. I want the freedom to wear as little as I care to. While I do not go as far as Ku Ch'ienli, the famous scholar who read the classics naked, I must be allowed to go half naked in my own room when the temperature is ninety-five in the shade, and I shall not be ashamed to appear so before my servants. I want them to be as natural beings as myself. I want a shower bath in summer and a good fireside with logs burning in winter.

I want a home where I can be myself. I want to hear my

wife's voice and the children's laughter upstairs when I am working downstairs, and downstairs when I am working upstairs. I want children who are children, who will go with me to play in the rain, and who enjoy a shower bath as much as I do. I want a patch of ground where my children can build brick houses and feed chickens and water flowers. I want to hear a cock crying cock-a-doodle-do in the morning. I want tall, old trees in the neighborhood.

I want some good friends, friends who are as familiar as life itself, friends to whom I need not be polite, and who will tell me all their troubles, matrimonial or otherwise, who can quote Aristophanes and crack some dirty jokes, friends who are spiritually rich and who can talk dirt and philosophy with the same candor, friends who have definite hobbies and opinions about persons and things, who have their private beliefs and respect mine.

I want a good cook, who knows how to cook vegetables and make delicious soups. I want an old, old servant, who thinks I am a great man, but does not know where my greatness is.

I want a good library, some good cigars and a woman who understands and who leaves me free to do my work.

I want some bamboos in front of my study window, a rainy climate in summer, and a clear, blue sky in winter, like what we have in Peking. I want the freedom to be myself.

The Little Critic: Essays, Satires and Sketches on China (Second Series: 1933–1935), pp. 101–104

Only he who is not wanted by the public can be a carefree individual, and only he who is a carefree individual can be a happy human being.

The Importance of Living, p. 161

16

The glory of a shoemaker who has completed making a good proud pair of shoes! The bliss of a farmer who has successfully completed digging a marsh ditch! What mystic delight can excel the pleasure of a pair of stretched legs after a good day's work?

On the Wisdom of America, p. 217

I have always been impressed by the fact that the most studiously avoided subject in western philosophy is that of happiness. It would be wonderful if there existed a philosophy devoted entirely to a study of the aims, methods and possibilities of attaining happiness in this present life. Common sense tells us that happiness is what everybody is striving for, and yet with all the past and present wisdom of men no one has attempted to tell us how to get there. The goal of religion is salvation, not happiness. Philosophy occupies itself with truth, not happiness. Moralists talk about duty, not happiness. Those who have money to spend seek after pleasures, not happiness. Socialists, whose aim is the greatest happiness of the greatest number, occupy themselves with economics, not happiness. Lovers who have sometimes caught that blue bird, squeeze it too tightly for joy, and find it dead on their hands. The only man who knows about happiness is a man with a pipe in his mouth—if he would only write a book and tell people about it!

On the Wisdom of America, p. 209

. . . there seems to be a philosophic contradiction between being busy and being wise. Those who are wise won't be busy, and those who are too busy can't be wise. The wisest man is therefore he who loafs most gracefully.

The Importance of Living, p. 150

17

Material progress alone with an increasing materialism does not necessarily make the modern man happier.

The Pleasures of a Nonconformist, p. 30

Most of us are happiest when we get a lot of mail and when we go to the movie theater and when we are in company.

On the Wisdom of America, p. 210

The ideal character best able to enjoy life is a warm, carefree and unafraid soul. Mencius enumerated the three "mature virtues" of his "great man" as "wisdom, compassion and courage." I should like to lop off one syllable and regard as the qualities of a great soul passion, wisdom and courage.

The Importance of Living, p. 98

I must confess to a secret partiality for the one who dreams. Generally he is the sadder one, but no matter; he is also capable of greater joys and thrills and heights of ecstasy.

The Importance of Living, p. 74

Very much contented am I to lie low, to cling to the soil, to be of kin to the sod. My soul squirms comfortably in the soil and sand and is happy. Sometimes when one is drunk with this earth, one's spirit seems so light that he thinks he is in heaven.

The Importance of Living, p. vii

I believe no one can be natural and happy unless he is intellectually sincere with himself, and to be natural is to be in heaven.

The Importance of Living, pp. 400–401

18

Peace of mind is that mental condition in which you have accepted the worst.

The Importance of Living, p. 403

If there is greater happiness than lying in the sun, I'd like to be told.

On the Wisdom of America, p. 220

After all allowances are made for the necessity of having a few supermen in our midst—explorers, conquerors, great inventors, great presidents, heroes who change the course of history—the happiest man is still the man of the middle-class who has earned a slight means of economic independence, who has done a little, but just a little, for mankind, and who is slightly distinguished in his community, but not too distinguished.

The Importance of Living, p. 115

"For me, a good mattress is very desirable. But when I have that, I am the equal of anybody: the world's richest millionaire does not sleep on a bigger mattress because he is a millionaire. His bed cannot be longer than mine, save a matter of inches. Nature makes us equal. The short span of life makes us equal. Old age and death make us equal. Death is democratic. Because Nature is democratic. An ulcer-free stomach may be all a millionaire will pray for. Nature compensates. Man imagines there are numberless things he wants. It is not true. He wants them only because he does not have them; when he has them, he does not want them. Pleasures grow stale. So as far as material well-being and happiness are concerned, there are only a few things."

Looking Beyond, p. 231

19

I am such a materialist that at any time I would prefer pork to poetry, and would waive a piece of philosophy for a piece of filet, brown and crisp and garnished with good sauce.

The Importance of Living, p. 143

We do not know a nation until we know its pleasures of life, just as we do not know a man until we know how he spends his leisure. It is when a man ceases to do the things he has to do, and does the things he likes to do, that his character is revealed. It is when the repressions of society and business are gone and when the goads of money and fame and ambition are lifted, and man's spirit wanders where it listeth, that we see the inner man, his real self. Life is harsh and politics is dirty and commerce is sordid, so that it would often be unfair to judge a man by his public life. For this reason, I find so many of our political scoundrels are such lovable human beings, and so many of our futile bombastic college presidents extremely good fellows at home.

My Country and My People, p. 322

. . . the wisdom of life consists in the elimination of non-essentials, in reducing the problems of philosophy to just a few —the enjoyment of the home (the relationship between man and woman and child), of living, of Nature and of culture—and in showing all the other irrelevant scientific disciplines and futile chases after knowledge to the door.

The Importance of Living, p. 10

Many men are happy in their ambition for power and success—another form of mild insanity which in the case of people

20

like Hitler assumes maniac proportions; many think of themselves as most important when two desk phones are ringing at the same time; many others rush from one international conference to another, making believe that they are experienced and wise enough to tackle the world's problems and leaving them very much where they were before, if they are lucky. Invariably, they create more problems for the world than they ever solve.

The Pleasures of a Nonconformist, p. 21

It is axiomatic that among the inmates of an insane asylum you never find a successful carrot-grower.

On the Wisdom of America, p. 225

When a man gets frightened or unhappy about the United Nations or the problems of world peace, and wants to recover his happiness, the best thing to do is to find some choked kitchen drain and try to clear it. There is hardly a man on earth who is not proud when he sees the water go down the sink smoothly with a clear gurgle as the result of his morning's labor. Or, instead of committing suicide over the tragedy of Czechoslovakia, one should find out if there isn't a shaky chair in the house and see if he can't fix it and make it safe to sit on again. After all, one can save the future of Czechoslovakia only by saving oneself and keeping oneself happy and alive first. The sovereign remedy for world chaos seems to be to provide every household with a hammer and a monkey wrench and a plentiful supply of nails.

On the Wisdom of America, p. 216

21

To some, eating is an adventure, a perpetual discovery of new flavors, unknown delights; to others it is merely a drab necessity of stifling hunger with any solids and fluids.

The Pleasures of a Nonconformist, p. 123

What a world of beauty is waiting for us, if we learn to wake up at dawn and listen to the heavenly concert of the birds!

The Importance of Living, p. 205

In this world of ours, happiness is very often negative, the complete absence of sorrow or mortification or bodily ailment. But happiness can also be positive, and then we call it joy. To me, for instance, the truly happy moments are: when I get up in the morning after a night of perfect sleep and sniff the morning air and there is an expansiveness in the lungs, when I feel inclined to inhale deeply and there is a fine sensation of movement around the skin and muscles of the chest, and when, therefore, I am fit for work; or when I hold a pipe in my hand and rest my legs on a chair, and the tobacco burns slowly and evenly; or when I am traveling on a summer day, my throat parched with thirst, and I see a beautiful clear spring, whose very sound makes me happy, and I take off my socks and shoes and dip my feet in the delightful, cool water; or when after a perfect dinner I lounge in an armchair, when there is no one I hate to look at in the company and conversation rambles off at a light pace to an unknown destination, and I am spiritually and physically at peace with the world; or when on a summer afternoon I see black clouds gathering on the horizon and know for certain a July shower is coming in a quarter of an hour, but being ashamed to be seen going out into the rain without an umbrella, I hastily set out to meet the shower halfway across the fields and come home drenched through and through and tell my family that I was simply caught by the rain.

The Importance of Living, pp. 126–127

If one's bowels move, one is happy, and if they don't move, one is unhappy. That is all there is to it.

The Importance of Living, p. 126

. . . no one's life can be happy unless beyond the superficial attainments of the external life, the deeper springs of his or her character are touched and find a normal outlet.

The Importance of Living, p. 173

The staid business man who is proud that he does not grow sentimental over an ordinary sun going down—does he not cry sometimes, cry for joy when his stocks jump up one hundred per cent in a day, or cry out of despair when the banks are closing his credit?

Confucius Saw Nancy and Essays About Nothing, p. 51

. . . happiness is peace, peace of body and peace of mind. It is a condition of satisfaction with oneself and with the surrounding one finds oneself in, and perhaps with one's purpose in life.

On the Wisdom of America, p. 214

There is always plenty of life to enjoy for a man who is determined to enjoy it. If men fail to enjoy this earthly existence we have, it is because they do not love life sufficiently and allow it to be turned into a humdrum routine existence. Laotse has been wrongly accused of being hostile to life; on the other hand, I think he taught the renunciation of the life of the world exactly because he loved life all too tenderly, to allow the art of living to degenerate into a mere business of living.

The Importance of Living, p. 155

So much of human life and happiness is subjective that we should be fools not to take advantage of this subjectivity unashamedly and learn to cultivate the seeing eye and the perceptive soul for the beauties that lie around us, and be grateful for it. Of all human vices, the greatest is ingratitude, and we must conclude that the world looks sick because the soul looking on it is sick. Any day, be it shine or rain or snow or a fearful storm, one cannot look out of the window without at least aesthetically feeling the beauty. Let it be raindrops dribbling down a windowpane, or the soft crack of hail upon the glass, or flying leaves, or a sparrow escaping from the storm outside, or the silent fall of the morning sunlight upon a corner of the carpet, or the shimmering outline of a retreating shadow—such ordinary phenomena should rout a man from his mood of pessimism and make him feel ashamed for being less than a dog, which usually knows how to adjust itself to circumstances quite competently. If life is all subjective, why not be subjectively happy rather than subjectively sad?

On the Wisdom of America, p. 155

All animals seem perfectly happy because all animals have their wants satisfied and provided by nature—or they die. The problem of human happiness comes up only because man has more complicated wants, perhaps an ambition, a desire to find a life purpose, and these wants are less easy to satisfy.

On the Wisdom of America, p. 215

Happiness has always seemed like a blue bird, and consists of moments. Such moments when we can be positive about being happy are, for instance, when we have had a really good dinner, when a friend we haven't seen for a long time suddenly turns up to chat for a whole evening, when a couple marches up the aisle to the wedding altar, when we have cleared all debts and after paying the income tax find there is still a comfortable margin left, when we hear that a wicked man has died or that we have the good opinion of somebody we respect, when we have spent a day of successful labor and our eyes feel drowsy and our muscles are pleasantly tired and there is no guest to prevent us from straightway going to bed. A moment later, happiness may be gone, and we start chasing it again. The bride driving away with her husband at the wheel may have a sudden unaccountable misgiving or even fear. The friend who has turned up seems changed, and there is an all but detectable decrease in his enthusiasm for life. The good opinion of our neighbor does not seem so reassuring when we search our hearts in the dead of the night. As for clearing all debts, you thought you had a fair margin left, but you had forgotten an item of $175.65. With the single exception of the man with the pleasantly tired muscles after a good day's work, not one is assured of a sound sleep that night. The very excitement of the occasion is disturbing and the human mind starts wondering again, thinks up imperfections, makes comparisons, and the man is saved and falls into a sound sleep only if he possesses a philosophy to laugh at himself. That is about the point where philosophy comes in.

If there could be a science of human happiness, I firmly believe that it should begin by being merely descriptive, contenting itself with describing or cataloguing our moments of happiness before analyzing them and drawing conclusions as to what makes men happy. One might learn to be open-minded, not caring what conclusion it leads to. I think that proceeding in this manner, one might have a fairly reliable guide as to what happiness is and how to attain it. If we reject a pompous theoretical approach and are objective and observant, we may be amazed to find, at the very first effort at thinking, that happiness is a common portion of our daily life, instead of the mysterious riddle which it is supposed to be. For instance, we might catch ourselves saying "I am happy" when we eat well. Such an observation of our commonest moments might lead to an important discovery of the source and nature of true happiness. The wise old Preacher of the Old Testament who certainly had made an experiment with life in search of happiness and had even "made a test of folly and madness" stumbled upon the same conclusion. "Therefore go, eat thy bread with joy, and drink thy wine with a merry heart." He had found that women failed him. If he was King Solomon, with his three thousand wives, I can understand why.

On the Wisdom of America, pp. 213–214

The pleasure of walking, of putting one leg forward, then the other, while requiring no skill, has a pleasure of smooth rhythm, of calming satisfaction, of intensified activity of the lungs and the whole bodily system, which is more allied to tea and tobacco as a means of spiritual comfort and release. In addition, of course, there is always the charm of the untrodden path, the smell of the hedgerow and the distant view of hills, or a meandering river or peaceful forests, as the case may be.

On the Wisdom of America, p. 267

There is a great probability that our loss of capacity for enjoying the positive joys of life is largely due to the decreased sensibility of our senses and our lack of full use of them.

The Importance of Living, pp. 127–128

26

We who put on dog collars and neckties and go with the regimented herd to an office every day cannot help envying a man who wears an old broad-brimmed hat and open shirt and a pair of shoes somewhat down at the heels, who dares to walk in the sun in the good hours of the morning, biting on a piece of straw between his lips and doing nothing. He is the man who does not yield to social pressures. He does not, at twenty-five, worry about old-age pensions. He does not have his annual holidays rationed; he takes them. Irresponsible, perhaps, but charming, reminding us of what we have lost. He is jealous of his personal liberty and a little disdainful of the multifarious activities of society and politics. He stands a little aloof and is not intimidated. Society does not approve, but he bares his crown to the sky and plants his feet on the earth and is unafraid. In the end, he is closer to the image as God once created him, and less like a caricature which society has made of us. That spirit of defiance at all conventional forms and manners, represented as it is by such an uninspiring symbol, is nevertheless the last best hope of earth and the fortress of democracy against totalitarian regimentation.

The Pleasures of a Nonconformist, p. 19

I always get a satirical delight in seeing a philosopher suffering from a tooth-ache and an optimistic poet suffering from dyspepsia.

The Importance of Living, pp. 27–28

It is the man who does not expect too much who is always happy. "One who is contented is always happy," says Laotse; and again, "one who is contented never fails." "A hot bowl of porridge on a cold winter morning is a great thing," says the painter Cheng Panch'iao. That hot bowl of porridge, two meals of rice with pickled turnips and a glimpse of meat lending flavor to the green

27

vegetables; an old cotton gown, a hard-working wife and disciplined children, and peace in the country—the Chinaman never prays for anything better. Because he expects so little from life, he is never disappointed, and because he knows always it can be worse, he is quite convinced that what is regarded as "bad" is not so bad after all.

The New York Times Magazine, November 14, 1937, p. 17

Happy is the man who is not confused, who still believes in a few simple truths and retains some simple faiths.

The Pleasures of a Nonconformist, p. 27

. . . happiness is the greatest of all moral virtues.

The Importance of Living, p. 232

The object of a dinner is not to eat and drink, but to join in merry-making and to make a lot of noise.

The Importance of Living, p. 247

A strong determination to get the best out of life, a keen desire to enjoy what one has, and no regrets if one fails; this is the secret of the Chinese genius for contentment.

My Country and My People, p. 66

It is all a frame of mind, this enjoyment of living. Wine may be the means of drowning sorrow, or a matter of habitual craving, or the proper occasion for feeling just a little elated, a little better than usual. Things don't give us anything except what we bring to the enjoyment of them. One may be a habitual cynic, taking pleasure in his cynicism, or a shallow optimist, or a sentimentalist, each frame of mind being as subjective as the others. How to select our spectacles through which to look at life is all a matter of personal choice. A frame of mind may become habitual and fixed, and then it becomes for that man a philosophy of life, an attitude toward it. A wise man would be careful not to let any particular frame of mind settle down into a permanent attitude, knowing that once he has got it, he will take a stubborn pleasure in it. A crusty old fool will delight in being just a crusty old fool, and a young sophisticated cynic will wallow in his cynicism.

On the Wisdom of America, pp. 229–230

. . . tea is invented for quiet company as wine is invented for a noisy party. There is something in the nature of tea that leads us into a world of quiet contemplation of life. It would be . . . disastrous to drink tea with babies crying around. . . .

The Importance of Living, p. 224

I believe one of the greatest pleasures of life is to curl up one's legs in bed. The posture of the arms is also very important, in order to reach the greatest degree of aesthetic pleasure and mental power. I believe the best posture is not lying flat on the bed, but being upholstered with big soft pillows at about thirty degrees with either one arm or both arms placed behind the back of the head. In this posture any poet could write immortal poetry, any philosopher could revolutionize human thought, and any scientist could make epoch-making discoveries.

Confucius Saw Nancy and Essays About Nothing, p. 54

29

". . . during the past two hundred years man has been thinking furiously and very successfully about matter, but very little about man, and the opportunity to live the good life has been lost."

Looking Beyond, p. 171

The only test of a soul's salvation is its inward happiness.

A Nun of Taishan and Other Translations, p. v

社會及文明

2
ON SOCIETY
AND
CIVILIZATION

᛭᛭

. . . the most bewildering thing about man is his idea of work and the amount of work he imposes upon himself, or civilization has imposed upon him. All nature loafs, while man alone works for a living. He works because he has to, because with the progress of civilization life gets incredibly more complex, with duties, responsibilities, fears, inhibitions and ambitions, born not of nature, but of human society.

The Importance of Living, p. 145

The difference between cannibals and civilized men seems to be that cannibals kill their enemies and eat them, while civilized men kill their foes and bury them, put a cross over their bodies and offer up prayers for their souls. Thus we add stupidity to conceit and a bad temper.

The Importance of Living, p. 50

No voice should cry in the wilderness; a man should come back and talk simply and sweetly and make peace with human society, if that vision he had seen in the desert was truly apocalyptic. I have sometimes wondered what that golden mean is that should mark the harmonious man. It is perhaps to be individualistic without being querulous, and to be urbane without truckling to conventions.

On the Wisdom of America, p. 161

We are all children of our age; we think and feel and buy and sell like men of our age.

The Pleasures of a Nonconformist, p. 21

". . . we are not so far from savagery so long as war is not abolished, however civilized we may think ourselves to be. . . . What difference is there between throwing a Christian to the lions in the arena and sending a son freshly graduated from college to be stabbed or blown to bits on the battlefield? What difference? A professional gladiator had a better chance against a lion than a grocer's son against the crackle and spitting fire of a machine gun. We believe that we are civilized and superior to the Romans only because we are not that grocer's son. Once you identify yourself with that grocer's boy, you don't think so. . . . It is possible only by the grossest lack of imagination on the part of the stay-at-homes to maintain the illusion of human civilization."

Looking Beyond, pp. 373–374

Modern civilization would be destroyed if the things that make for civilization, the things we take for granted—freedom of belief, the rights and liberties of the individual, democracy, and that now tottering faith in the common man—if these things were destroyed.

The New York Times Magazine, November 12, 1939, p. 2

34

Freedom of the press is a mockery, in spite of big circulations, unless there is the freedom to squeal when hurt, a benefit of civilization now enjoyed only by the animal kingdom less mankind.

A History of the Press and Public Opinion in China, p. 1

. . . if we could recapture a day, a moment, and reveal its full meaning and hold it in true focus, we might be good historians of that epoch, as so mirrored in the way men and women eat and dress and live and think about the tomorrow.

The Vigil of a Nation, p. 6

. . . I find grand old men with white beards missing in the American picture. I know that they exist, but they are perhaps in a conspiracy to hide themselves from me.

The Importance of Living, p. 198

We love old cathedrals, old furniture, old silver, old dictionaries and old prints, but we have entirely forgotten about the beauty of old men. I think an appreciation of that kind of beauty is essential to our life, for beauty, it seems to me, is what is old and mellow and well-smoked.

The Importance of Living, p. 165

It would be insane to look for public order where private anarchy exists.

On the Wisdom of America, p. 38

". . . I believe world civilization can be built only upon the common basis of international living, a combination of all that is best and finest in each civilization. The ideal life would be, I think, to live in an English cottage, with American heating, and have a Japanese wife, a French mistress and a Chinese cook."

Looking Beyond, p. 201

Few men who have liberated themselves from the fear of God and the fear of death are yet able to liberate themselves from the fear of man. Consciously or unconsciously, we are all actors in this life playing to the audience in a part and style approved by them.

The Importance of Living, p. 104

The first condition of learning how to eat is to talk about it. Only in a society wherein people of culture and refinement inquire after their cooks' health, instead of talking about the weather, can the art of cuisine be developed. No food is really enjoyed unless it is keenly anticipated, discussed, eaten and then commented upon.

My Country and My People, p. 338

To glorify the past and paint the future is easy, to survey the present and emerge with some light and understanding is difficult.

My Country and My People, p. 349

. . . no man need forget that he is the end of all creation, that society and politics have no meaning except to keep him a tolerably free individual, with the rights of life, liberty, and the pursuit of happiness.

The Pleasures of a Nonconformist, p. 23

36

Perhaps the production of that individual who is most careful not to hurt others' feelings is the end of civilization; perhaps not—how can we know? But it is possible that to a man of the twenty-fifth century our social behavior as individuals and as nations may seem extremely uncouth, and some of the world leaders we are worshiping today may appear no more than barbarians with a tribalistic mind, as we think of Hannibal today.

The Atlantic Monthly, December, 1942, pp. 45-46

A human race endowed with gullets or gizzards would be found to have the most peaceful, contented and sweet nature, like the chicken or the lamb. . . . Not until we develop a gizzard temper can we call ourselves truly civilized.

The Importance of Living, pp. 49-50

. . . history reveals and the Confucian theory of imitation affirms that in times of national crisis it is the great men who change the destiny of a nation.

My Country and My People, p. 359

In every nation, the happiness of women does not depend on how many social advantages they enjoy, but on the quality of the men they live with.

My Country and My People, p. 147

In this present age of threats to democracy and individual liberty, probably only the scamp and the spirit of the scamp alone will save us from becoming lost as serially numbered units in the masses of disciplined, obedient, regimented and uniformed coolies. The scamp will be the last and most formidable enemy of dictatorships. He will be the champion of human dignity and individual freedom, and will be the last to be conquered. All modern civilizationdependsentirelyuponhim.

The Importance of Living, p. 12

In the progress of human civilization the arts of living and the arts of killing—artcraft and warcraft—have always existed side by side. No history of any nation shows that a period of peace without domestic or foreign wars ever existed for more than 300 years. This seems to derive from the fact that man is both a fighting and a peaceful animal. In him the fighting instinct and the instinct for peaceful living—which I call the carnivorous and the herbivorous instincts—are strangely mixed.

This is not to imply a state of human imperfection; it may be questioned whether the kind of civilization wherein man is so thoroughly tamed and domesticated that there is no more fight left in him would be worth having at all. Life is, or should be, accompanied by struggle, or else the racial fiber degenerates, which happens within the amazingly short period of a few generations in a well-provided family.

I am not trying to condone war, but am merely pointing out our biological heritage. In the world of nature the warring instinct and the instinct to live are different aspects of the same thing. Those primeval biological instincts go deeper than any temporary ideologies or political creeds. In the biological world merciless wars have always existed side by side with the most persistent displays of love for the young and all those manifestations of courtship which produce beauty and which we know as the charm and fragrance of the flower, the caroling of the lark and the song of the cricket.

The New York Times Magazine, November 12, 1939, p. 1

Speaking as a Chinese, I do not think that any civilization can be called complete until it has progressed from sophistication to unsophistication, and made a conscious return to simplicity of thinking and living, and I call no man wise until he has made the progress from the wisdom of knowledge to the wisdom of foolishness, and become a laughing philosopher, feeling first life's tragedy and then life's comedy. For we must weep before we can laugh. Out of sadness comes the awakening and out of the awakening comes the laughter of the philosopher, with kindliness and tolerance to boot.

The Importance of Living, p. 13

. . . all great liberals of history are great nuisances.

The Little Critic: Essays, Satires and Sketches on China (First Series: 1930–1932), p. 109

No nation can go about conquering the world unless she is quite certain of her "civilizing" mission. The moment, however, that you begin to think and see something in the other nation or the other fellow and his ways, your moral conviction leaves you, and your empire collapses.

With Love and Irony, p. 8

No civilization has any excuse for depriving a man or woman of his or her right to have babies.

The Importance of Living, p. 168

"When the feminine ideal crumbles, civilization starts on its way to decay."

Looking Beyond, p. 311

39

The true test of a civilization is not how you are able to conquer and to kill but how you can get the greatest kick out of life.

With Love and Irony, pp. 14–15

The problem of leisure will remain the central problem of all civilization.

Asia, November, 1936, p. 744

We cannot escape history, nor can we learn from history.

Between Tears and Laughter, p. 126

Human civilization has changed so much that space is something that the average man cannot own and cannot have. We have gone so far that a man is entirely complacent when he owns a *mow* of civilized lawn, in the midst of which he succeeds in digging a five-foot pond to keep his goldfish and making a mound that would not take ants five minutes to crawl to the top. This has changed entirely our conception of the home. There is no more poultry yard, no well and no place where one's children can catch crickets and get comfortably dirty. Instead, our home becomes physically like a pigeon's house called an "apartment," with a combination of buttons, switches, cabinets, rubber mats, keyholes, wires and burglar-alarms which we call a home. There are no attics, no dirt and no spiders. Our perversion of the idea of a home has gone so far that some Western people are even proud of the fact that they sleep on a bed which is the back of a daytime sofa. They show it to their friends and marvel at modern technological civilization. The modern spiritual home is broken up because the physical home has disappeared, as Edward Sapir pointed out. People move into a three-room flat and then wonder why they can never keep their children at home.

My Country and My People, pp. 329–330

It has seemed to me that the final test of any civilization is, what type of husbands and wives and fathers and mothers does it turn out? Besides the austere simplicity of such a question, every other achievement of civilization—art, philosophy, literature and material living—pales into insignificance.

The Importance of Living, p. 166

The world is always better for men who have dreamed and who have dared to criticize what is sick and unhealthy in their times.

The Secret Name, pp. 221–222

To me, spiritually a child of the East and West, man's dignity consists in the following facts which distinguish man from animals. First, that he has a playful curiosity and a natural genius for exploring knowledge; second, that he has dreams and a lofty idealism (often vague, or confused, or cocky, it is true, but nevertheless worthwhile); third, and still more important, that he is able to correct his dreams by a sense of humor, and thus restrain his idealism by a more robust and healthy realism; and finally, that he does not react to surroundings mechanically and uniformly as animals do, but possesses the ability and the freedom to determine his own reactions and to change surroundings at his will.

The Importance of Living, pp. 11–12

41

The great thing about the teaching of history is that we must teach history but must not let history teach us.

Between Tears and Laughter, p. 9

Men of character and ability and moral rectitude are rare products of a civilized society and thus take a long time to grow up and mature.

The Gay Genius, p. 384

The humor of the Chinese people in inventing gunpowder and finding its best use in making firecrackers for their grandfathers' birthdays is merely symbolical of their inventiveness along merely pacific lines.

My Country and My People, p. 24

. . . we cannot produce a Moses or a Confucius in the modern age.

The Nation, May 6, 1939, p. 528

". . . the meek shall inherit the earth, but they will no longer be meek when they have come into the inheritance."

Looking Beyond, p. 96

"When you come to chalk up the progress of human civilization, you suddenly realize that tobacco and wine and the lyre are among the very few important permanent discoveries of mankind, the real, definite gains for human comfort and wise, genial living."

Looking Beyond, p. 82

No civilization can exist without some fairly stable ideas of man, his history, God, the soul, the universe, and the purpose of man's existence. These ideas, as far as I can make out, are in a state of rather disgraceful confusion, disgraceful for a twentieth-century man who boasts of his great progress.

On the Wisdom of America, p. 37

Miserable indeed is a world in which we have knowledge without understanding, criticism without appreciation, beauty without love, truth without passion, righteousness without mercy, and courtesy without a warm heart!

The Importance of Living, p. 142

"The distinction between civilization and culture is not easy. These words, like all words, grew in their meaning through usage. I would say that civilization refers more to our material advances, culture to the spiritual gains . . . I think a man can be civilized without being cultured. The advances and gains of civilization are physical, they are something added extraneously to the man; culture's influence is chemical, it enters into the man's inner being and changes him."

Looking Beyond, p. 200

. . . it is not dirt but the fear of dirt which is the sign of man's degeneration.

My Country and My People, p. 23

43

A scientist can hide behind his fortress of objectivity and do the world no harm while he is studying rocks. But when a student of human society and human psychology hides behind such a fortress of objectivity, regarding praise or condemnation as being of no concern of his, he inevitably leads the way to a void of values, whether he wants to or not. And when such a mode of thinking becomes general or even fashionable, society must increasingly tend to lose all convictions.

Now all the academic jargon of the psychologists and sociologists reveals a desire to appear scientific, and a desire to understand, but not to evaluate moral significances. I may be old-fashioned, but I think it will be a long time before you will hear an educational psychologist dare to say that a child's behavior is "right" or "wrong," "selfish" or "unselfish." To say that a certain type of behavior is right or wrong would be to imply lack of objectivity, a tendency to condemn or praise, which is none of science's business. The phrase "a selfish person" implies condemnation, but the phrase "a maladjusted individual" does not. Therefore when a person is selfish, he is merely maladjusted. And so we go on to "patterns of behavior," "Oedipus complex," "emotional instability," "childhood inhibitions," "atavism," straight down to "amnesia," "split personality," and "temporary insanity," the last of which can and does excuse murder. The emphasis is always toward placing the blame either on heredity or on environment, never on the will and the responsibility of the individual. If the newspapers would agree to stop using the phrase "juvenile delinquency" and start using "young lawbreaker" or "young criminal" instead, we could probably cut youthful crime by 50 per cent. Obviously, no teen-age boy minds being called a juvenile delinquent, which is of Latin origin and charmingly colorless and remote, but every one of them—I have seen such "juveniles" standing six foot tall on the pavements of Manhattan —hates to be branded a "young criminal." The psychologist means to say that he is an unfortunate victim of circumstances

44

and is juvenile and temporarily delinquent, and does not know right from wrong. I think that these six-foot fellows know very well what is right and what is wrong, and know exactly what they are doing when they murder or rob. Any Asiatic boy of twelve knows what is right and what is wrong, and to say that an American boy of sixteen or seventeen still does not know right from wrong (and therefore has no moral responsibility for his actions) is an obvious travesty of the American people, and implies immaturity on the part of the adolescent "social scientists." A socially maladjusted individual is not just a socially maladjusted individual; he is, in plain English, just an ill-bred brat. Now the human constitution is such that if you call a brat a brat, the brat disappears; but if you call an ill-bred shuffling sneak or shirker of duties just an emotionally unbalanced personality, he rather likes it and is proud of it and wears his hair and his dress in a manner to advertise it.

From Pagan to Christian pp. 218–220

In every age and every period of history, after every war and every revolution, Liberty and Reaction go side by side together and struggle for supremacy for the moment.

Between Tears and Laughter, p. 35

"All cooks talk a language which the different nations can understand."

Looking Beyond, p. 199

Degeneration is a highly misleading term, for it can only be relative in meaning. Since the invention of the flush toilet and the vacuum carpet cleaner, the modern man seems to judge a man's moral standards by his cleanliness, and thinks a dog the more highly civilized for having a weekly bath and a winter wrapper round his belly. . . . The dog which remembers only to bark and not to bite, and is led through the streets as a lady's pet, is only a degenerate wolf.

My Country and My People, p. 23

. . . order is seldom exciting.

The Wisdom of Laotse, p. 4

. . . we are no longer called upon to adapt ourselves to nature; we are called upon to adapt ourselves to ourselves, to this thing called civilization. All instincts were good, were healthy in nature; in society, however, we call all instincts savage. Every mouse steals —and he is not the less moral or more immoral for stealing— every dog barks, every cat doesn't come home at night and tears everything it can lay its paws upon, every lion kills, every horse runs away from the sight of danger, every tortoise sleeps the best hours of the day away, and every insect, reptile, bird and beast reproduces its kind in public. Now in terms of civilization, every mouse is a thief, every dog makes too much noise, every cat is an unfaithful husband, when he is not a savage little vandal, every lion or tiger is a murderer, every horse a coward, every tortoise a lazy louse, and finally, every insect, reptile, bird and beast is obscene when he performs his natural vital functions. What a wholesale transformation of values! And that is the reason why we sit back and wonder how the Lord made us so imperfect.

The Importance of Living, p. 37

Our contrary-mindedness is our only hope for civilization. My reason is simple: that we are descended from the monkeys and

46

not from the cows, and that therefore we are better monkeys, nobler monkeys, for being contrary-minded. I am selfish enough as a human being to desire a sweet and contented temper for the cows, who can be led to the pasture or to the slaughter-house at human behest with equal magnanimity and nobility of mind, motivated by the sole desire to sacrifice themselves for their master. At the same time, I am such a lover of humanity as not to desire that we become cows ourselves. The moment cows rebel and feel our recalcitrancy, or begin to act waywardly and less mechanically, I call them human. The reason I think all dictatorships are wrong is a biological reason. Dictators and cows go well together, but dictators and monkeys don't.

The Importance of Living, p. 84

Anybody who will speak the truth about society is bound to shock the world.

The Little Critic: Essays, Satires and Sketches on China (Second Series: 1933–1935), pp. 225–226

Everybody has been tamed by society; everybody has become "nice" and socially acceptable and "knowledgeable."

The Pleasures of a Nonconformist, p. 23

I am inclined to think that the man who sits on a chair that is a real chair, and sleeps on a bed that is a real bed (and not a daytime sofa) is a happier man. The standard that measures a man's civilization by the number of mechanical buttons he presses in a day must, therefore, be a false standard.

My Country and My People, p. 62

LIN YUTANG: THE BEST OF AN OLD FRIEND

"All utopias . . . presume too much upon human nature, and therefore must fail. It's very easy for a man to write a book and say, I don't like human nature this way—all right, I'll change it. Karl Marx is one of them. A classless society in which the state withers! We have seen in practice how his followers found it necessary to erect the most despotic state known to history—just to enable those in authority to remain in power. A classless society united in brotherly love and devoted to the public good! Parent-child affection will be replaced by a higher kind of loyalty! Men will work for the love of the state, not for profit! That is where Marx went completely nutty. Any time man plays a trick on Nature, Nature plays a nasty trick in return, and exacts payment with double interest."

Looking Beyond, p. 47

Man is taught to admire beautiful things, not by books but by social example, and by living in a society of good taste.

My Country and My People, p. 323

The home is the training ground of one's character. If good manners are to be learned, they must be learned at home. If patience and forbearance and tolerance are to be learned, they must be learned at home. If men are to be taught to behave in society like civilized people, they must be taught at home. The man who loves the whole world but cannot get along with his own parents evidently is a very badly adjusted individual. He just never learned to adjust himself in his close personal relationships.

The Pleasures of a Nonconformist, p. 75

48

There are a rhythm and a pattern of things in human history if only we could detect them.

Between Tears and Laughter, p. 17

A society without a philosophy of life is a frightening thing.

On the Wisdom of America, p. xii

Against Plato, I must say that laziness is the mother of inventions. It is so easy to switch on an electric light, so messy to clean and light a kerosene lamp. Without human laziness it would be inconceivable that electric light should replace the oil lamp. It was human indolence that invented the carriage in place of walking. The elevator is an unashamed appeal to human laziness in climbing the stairs. It is human laziness that makes us prefer running water from the faucet to carrying pails of water to the house. Above all, laziness is the backbone of the cigarette industry; few men nowadays care to roll their own cigarettes, but buy them ready made, light them, and then leave them burning in the ashtray. It is so comfortable to be lazy. I doubt that without laziness any of the modern comforts could have been invented. Now you press a button and the automobile window slides up or down automatically. How blessed are we with this extraordinary gift of a desire to do the greatest amount of work with the least expenditure of energy! Without laziness in our bones, where would civilization be today?

The Pleasures of a Nonconformist, p. 32

This is the value of historical study, that it teaches us to see the present in the past . . .

A History of the Press and Public Opinion in China, p. 46

49

. . . the meek shall always win and shall inherit the earth, when the earth is at last civilized.

The Pleasures of a Nonconformist, p. 81

Every nation dreams, and acts more or less completely on her dreams. Human history is the result of the conflict of our ideals and realities, and the adjustment between ideals and reality determines the peculiar development of that nation.

With Love and Irony, p. 4

Any man or boy who professes indifference to a Mickey Mouse cartoon is decidedly a mental degenerate and can be of no use to civilization. Generally, it is the man who has many wants and desires and hopes that lives a richer and more complete life, not the one who goes on in life, indifferent to what is around him.

The Little Critic: Essays, Satires and Sketches on China (Second Series: 1933–1935), p. 100

Man in the country does not degenerate; only man in the cities does.

My Country and My People, p. 36

. . . a civilization which ignores the home or relegates it to a minor position is apt to turn out poorer products.

The Importance of Living, p. 167

It seems that in the present age of rising collectivism of all sorts—social, economic and political—mankind is naturally forgetting and forfeiting its right to human recalcitrancy and losing sight of the dignity of the individual. With the predominance of economic problems and economic thinking, which is overshadowing all other forms of human thinking, we remain completely ignorant of, and indifferent to, a more humanized knowledge and a more humanized philosophy, a philosophy that deals with the problems of the individual life. This is natural. As a man who has an ulcered stomach spends all his thought on his stomach, so a society with a sick and aching economics is forever preoccupied with thoughts of economics. Nevertheless, the result is that we remain totally indifferent to the individual and have almost forgotten that he exists. A man used to be a man for a'that. Today he is generally conceived as an automaton blindly obeying material or economic laws. We no longer think of a man as a man, but as a cog in a wheel, a member of a union or a class, an alien to be imported by quotas, a *petit bourgeois* to be referred to with contempt, or a capitalist to be denounced, or a worker to be regarded as a comrade because he is a worker. It seems that to label a man as a *petit bourgeois* or a "capitalist" or a "worker" is already to understand him completely, and he can be conveniently hated or hailed as a comrade accordingly. We are no longer individuals, no longer men, but only classes. May I suggest that this is an oversimplification of things? The scamp has completely disappeared as an ideal, and so has the man with his gloriously scamp-like qualities of reacting freely and incalculably to his external surroundings. Instead of men, we have members of a class; instead of ideas and personal prejudices and idiosyncracies, we have ideologies, or class thoughts; instead of personalities, we have blind forces; and instead of individuals, we have a Marxian dialectic controlling and foreshadowing all human activities with unfailing precision. We are all progressing happily and enthusiastically toward the model of the ants.

The Importance of Living, pp. 85–86

You cannot make a philosophic individualist into a good citizen.

With Love and Irony, p. 37

Social action follows naturally from a good family breeding. Learn to be a good child at home, a good son, and a good brother, and all the other goods will be added unto you.

From Pagan to Christian, p. 93

The constant rush for progress must certainly one day reach a point when man will be pretty tired of it all, and will begin to take stock of his conquests in the material world. I cannot believe that, with the coming of better material conditions of life, when diseases are eliminated, poverty is decreased and man's expectation of life is prolonged and food is plentiful, man will care to be as busy as he is today. I'm not so sure that a more lazy temperament will not arise as a result of this new environment.

The Importance of Living, p. 149

The quality of men and women we live with is much more important than the work they achieve. . . .

The Importance of Living, p. 167

Civilization does not degenerate till it begins to adore effeminate living.

On the Wisdom of America, p. 272

. . . the western view of the nature, function, and aim of human life is almost 95 per cent economic.

Between Tears and Laughter, p. 61

Yes, real or not, we have to take the world as it is and man as he is without demanding perfection and then damning him for what the theologians think he should be but is not.

On the Wisdom of America, p. 23

3
ON
GAINING
PERSPECTIVE

ᵚᵚ
ᵚᵚ

While not living a saint's life, I believe I have lived a fairly decent human life. Legally I am perfect, while morally I have imperfections. But all these moral imperfections or delinquencies, like occasional lying and neglect of duty, added up together and placed before my mother as the judge, would probably make me deserve a three years' imprisonment at the most, but certainly not the damnation of hell-fire. This is not boasting; few of my friends deserve five years at the worst.

The Nation, May 6, 1939, p. 527

Imagine a world in which there are no stories of murder in newspapers, everyone is so omniscient that no house ever catches fire, no airplane ever has an accident, no husband deserts his wife, no pastor elopes with a choir girl, no king abdicates his throne for love, no man changes his mind and everyone proceeds to carry out with logical precision a career that he mapped out for himself at the age of ten—good-by to this happy human world! All the excitement and uncertainty of life would be gone. There would be no literature because there would be no sin, no misbehavior, no human weakness, no upsetting passion, no prejudices, no irregularities and, worst of all, no surprises.

The Importance of Living, p. 59

57

Apparently, in nature's scheme, there is not a blessing in this life without its concomitant evils, and not an evil without its compensatory blessings.

The Vigil of a Nation, p. 40

The unique and the exotic make such interesting after-dinner stories, while the central and common truths of humanity are forgotten.

My Country and My People, p. 148

I do not know whether I am more in dead earnest about light topics or in a lighter mood when dealing with serious ones. I have no sense of their relative importance.

The Pleasures of a Nonconformist, p. 11

So we are in this race of life, from childhood, manhood, to old age and death, colored by friendships, achievements, failures, and relative successes, followed by the imperceptible stealthy footsteps of time. It would be good to be able to say, "The years draw to a close and I am content." There is pathos and humor in it. Perhaps somewhere after forty, a wrinkle creeps up here and a straggling white hair puts in its appearance there, marking the approach of life's early autumn. Perhaps the symphony of autumn's colors is richer, more desperate, more flamboyant than that of summer, and we catch a little breath but know that this is the universal rhythm of life. How to fall in step with life's rhythms is perhaps the very center of a good philosophy of life, which can bring the peace of content. The hoop that we used to trundle as a boy has lost its charm, and certain marks of value, like

58

the college diploma or some ribbon or insignificant prize for which we fought with all our energies as if life itself depended on it, seem of as little worth as the pair of shoes we discarded long ago. We can even think with a little touch of irony and laughter of some of the foolish ambitions, the impossible ventures, the laudable fancies with which youth colored its own life. In middle age, streets seem narrower, great men seem commoner, and titles of office less impressive, while our opinions seem ever more and more assured, and we are apt to imagine ourselves fast approaching the infallibility of the pope, at least in our own homes. "Tut! Tut!" we say to every youth's young dream. "If you had lived as long as I have and seen as much. . . ." That is about the time to draw ourselves up and see the image of old age suddenly visible walking by our side as a companion. That is the time to flex our intellectual muscles, draw a deep breath, and change directions.

On the Wisdom of America, p. 74

Every man and woman between thirty and forty gradually finds out what he or she really wants in this life, and sorts out the essentials from the nonessentials.

The Pleasures of a Nonconformist, p. 100

. . . since we are alike under the skin, what touches the human heart in one country touches all.

The Importance of Living, p. 1

All youth is idealistic, in all countries East or West. All youth is radical. All youth demands something to fight for and sacrifice for, and especially something to fight against, to tear down and destroy, something which calls for danger, adventure, blood, sweat and tears and camping in the open.

The Secret Name, p. 226

Once a farmer was going home after his day's work. On his way he had bought a pot of soybean sauce, and this he carried at the back end of a bamboo pole swing across his shoulder. The pot of soybean sauce slipped off the pole and crashed on the stone pavement, but the farmer walked on as if nothing had happened. A passenger thought he hadn't noticed it and called it to his attention. "I know," replied the farmer. "But if it's broken, it's broken, isn't it?" In the circumstances, there was just nothing to do about it. He didn't stop for it, and he didn't cry.

Asia, October, 1946, p. 453

When a man is young, he wants to get things and achieve things, but when a man grows older, he begins to see things in their right perspective. He becomes less aggressive and more pacifist; he is intent not on getting things but on keeping the things he has, the things of true value; he is less desirous to make progress than to know how to live.

The Little Critic: Essays, Satires and Sketches on China (Second Series: 1933–1935), p. 16

An American editor worries his hair gray to see that no typographical mistakes appear on the pages of his magazine. The Chinese editor is wiser than that. He wants to leave his readers the supreme satisfaction of discovering a few typographical mistakes for themselves. More than that, a Chinese magazine can begin printing serial fiction and forget about it halfway. In America it might bring the roof down on the editors, but in China *it doesn't matter, simply because it doesn't matter.* American engineers in building bridges calculate so finely and exactly as to make the two ends come together within one-tenth of an inch. But when two Chinese begin to dig a tunnel from both sides of a mountain, both come out on the other side. The Chinese's firm conviction is that it doesn't matter so long as a tunnel is dug through, and if we have two instead of one, why, we have a double track to boot. Provided you are not in a hurry, two tunnels are as good as one, dug somehow, finished somehow and if the train can get through somehow.

The Importance of Living, pp. 162–163

. . . no child is born with a really cold heart, and it is only in proportion as we lose that youthful heart that we lose the inner warmth in ourselves. Somewhere in our adult life, our sentimental nature is killed, strangled, chilled or atrophied by an unkind surrounding, largely through our own fault in neglecting to keep it alive, or our failure to keep clear of such surroundings. In the process of learning "world experience," there is many a violence done to our original nature, when we learn to harden ourselves, to be artificial, and often to be cold-hearted and cruel, so that as one prides oneself upon gaining more and more worldly experience, his nerves become more and more insensitive and benumbed—especially in the world of politics and commerce. As a result, we get the great "go-getter" pushing himself forward to the top and brushing everybody aside; we get the man of iron will and strong determination, with the last embers of sentiment, which he calls foolish idealism or sentimentality, gradually dying out in his breast. It is that sort of person who is beneath my contempt. The world has too many cold-hearted people. If sterilization of the unfit should be carried out as a state policy, it should begin with sterilizing the morally insensible, the artistically stale, the heavy of heart, the ruthlessly successful, the cold-heartedly deter-

61

mined and all those people who have lost the sense of fun in life —rather than the insane and the victims of tuberculosis. For it seems to me that while a man with passion and sentiment may do many foolish and precipitate things, a man without passion or sentiment is a joke and a caricature. Compared with Daudet's Sappho, he is a worm, a machine, an automaton, a blot upon this earth. Many a prostitute lives a nobler life than a successful business man. What if Sappho sinned? For although she sinned, she also loved, and to those who love much, much will be forgiven. Anyway she emerged out of an equally harsh business environment with more of the youthful heart than many of our millionaires. The worship of Mary Magdalene is right. It is unavoidable that passion and sentiment should lead us into mistakes for which we are duly punished, yet there is many an indulgent mother who by her indulgence often let her love get the better of her judgment, and yet who, we feel sure, in her old age felt that she had had a more happy life with her family than many rigorous and austere souls. A friend told me the story of an old lady of seventy-eight who said to him, "As I look back upon my seventy-eight years, it still makes me happy to think of when I sinned; but when I think I was stupid, I cannot forgive myself even at this late day."

The Importance of Living, pp. 100–101

Every Chinese is a good Confucianist when he is a success, but a Taoist when he is in trouble or frustrated and beset by difficulties and failures. As men more often fail than succeed, and even those who apparently succeed have secret doubts of their own in the middle of the night, the Taoist influence is more often at work than the Confucian. The official who has been kicked out of office immediately goes to a hot spring and plays with his children, and says to himself: "I am a free man once more! It is wonderful. That is how God intended man to live all along." This official probably used to suffer from insomnia when he was an important secretary at some ministry; now he sleeps well because he is sleeping in the bosom of the Taoist universe.

From Pagan to Christian, pp. 111–112

In what country does not youth like to be thought of as "progressive" and take a hand in upsetting something or other?

The Vigil of a Nation, p. 58

Nothing is very new which is not very old.

The Secret Name, p. 15

No one can really stop growing old; he can only cheat himself by not admitting that he is growing old. And since there is no use fighting against nature, one might just as well grow old gracefully. The symphony of life should end with a grand finale of peace and serenity and material comfort and spiritual contentment, and not with the crash of a broken drum or cracked cymbals.

The Importance of Living, p. 201

Man is liable to forget how small and often how futile he is. A man seeing a hundred-story building often gets conceited, and the best way to cure that insufferable conceit is to transport that skyscraper in one's imagination to a little contemptible hill and learn a truer sense of what may and what may not be called "enormous."

The Importance of Living, p. 282

The world will right itself. Take a long view and you are comforted.

The Nation, May 6, 1939, p. 530

. . . the world is full of people who have no depth and no originality and yet get on swimmingly.

With Love and Irony, p. 34

We can well take for granted that no one in the present generation, or only very few, are prudish; the trend is rather to the contrary. But the vast majority of men and women still have modesty, which cannot be simply talked away.

On the Wisdom of America, p. 383

. . . we all romanticize life and history according to our favorite individual points of view.

On the Wisdom of America, p. 446

Most of us believe that our own country is the best, our morals the highest and our religion the purest.

The Little Critic: Essays, Satires and Sketches on China (First Series: 1930–1932), p. 107

In youth and romance and love, the world is pretty much the same, only the psychological reactions differ as a result of different social traditions.

My Country and My People, p. 155

In real life, any woman would be grateful for being accepted as an ordinary human being, like any man, perhaps at most slightly raised on a two-inch heel, not much higher, and certainly not on a pedestal. It just won't work. Woman shares all man's foibles, all man's pettiness and vanity, as she shares all his hopes and ambitions. Woman is venal; woman is vain; woman is realistic. What do we take her for? An angel? The falsehood lies in the implication that man isn't all these things.

On the Wisdom of America, pp. 68–69

It is by no mere whim that, in Greek mythology, young Icarus was made to fly too high until the wax of his wings melted and he fell into the sea, while Daedalus, the old father, flew safe to the home land, but flew very much lower. When a man grows old, he develops a genius for flying low, and idealism is tempered with cool, level-headed common sense, as well as with a sense for pounds and shillings. Realism is, then, characteristic of old age, as idealism is characteristic of youth.

*The Little Critic: Essays, Satires and Sketches on China
(First Series: 1930–1932),* pp. 34–35

A person gets a kind of flavor from reading the *Book of Changes* at forty, and gets another kind of flavor reading it at fifty, after he has seen more changes in life.

The Importance of Living, p. 380

There is nothing that a man will not eat when hard pressed by hunger. And no one is entitled to condemn until he knows what famine means.

My Country and My People, p. 337

. . . life always looks different from an altitude of five thousand feet. People fond of horseback riding always say that the moment one goes up on horseback, one obtains a different view of the world. . . .

My Country and My People, p. 289

Nothing matters to a man who says nothing matters.

The Importance of Living, p. 161

It is really not so difficult to know a man dead a thousand years ago. Considering how incomplete our knowledge usually is of people who live in the same city with us, or even of the private life of the mayor, it seems sometimes easier to know a dead man than a living one. For one thing, the living man's life is not completed, and one never knows what he is going to do next when a crisis comes. The drunkard reforms, the saint falls, and the pastor runs away with a choir girl. A living man has always so many "possibilities." Then, too, the living man has secrets, and some of the best secrets usually come out long after the man is dead. That is why it is so difficult usually to judge a contemporary, whose life is too close to us.

The Gay Genius, p. 1

To understand the old is difficult, and to understand the new is not too easy.

My Country and My People, p. 280

Too much mental sanity often clips imagination of its wings and deprives the race of its moments of blissful madness; pacifism can become a vice of cowardice; patience, again, may bring about a morbid tolerance of evil; conservatism may at times be a mere synonym for sloth and laziness, and fecundity may be a racial virtue but an individual vice.

My Country and My People, pp. 43–44

. . . it is dangerous to judge a man's physical and moral sanity by outside standards.

My Country and My People, p. 23

Human history is not the product of the wise direction of human reason, but is shaped by the forces of emotion— our dreams, our pride, our greed, our fears, and our desire for revenge.

Confucius Saw Nancy and Essays About Nothing, p. 95

Never, never shall we come nearer to the truths of life than man did two thousand years ago. There is nothing new under the sun and too much study is a weariness of the flesh. The wisest of philosophers have knocked at the door of the universe in vain. The history of philosophy is a rehash of old truths. We nod and wake up and nod again.

On the Wisdom of America, p. 446

". . . excess of virtue is a vice."

Looking Beyond, pp. 149–150

When I took up a New York paper a few weeks ago and read that some astronomer had discovered a new star cluster 250,000 light-years away from the earth, my notion of man's place in nature became downright ridiculous. These things are not unimportant in their bearings on our belief; they are highly important. I long ago reached the point where I realized how small and puny and humble I looked in God's, or the universe's eyes, until the idea of a complicated system of downfall, punishment, and redemption seemed as absurd and preposterous to me as if I were to imagine myself evolving a system of punishment and redemption for a being less than the size of an ant's feeler, or even of a fair-sized maggot. We are individually not worth God's anger. We are not worth a damn, literally.

I Believe, p. 163

After the engineers have changed the face of the earth, men are very much the same as their forefathers were centuries ago.

The Pleasures of a Nonconformist, p. 30

The average human body looks either like a monkey or an overfed horse, and only clothes help some to look like colonels and others like bank presidents. Strip them and farewell to the colonels and the bank presidents! Their occasional nudism at home explains why they are generally thought beneath contempt by their wives. Strip the high and mighty delegates to international conferences naked, and we would have gained a truer insight into the present world chaos, being essentially ruled by monkeys. And strip Mussolini, Hitler and Stalin naked before their peoples, and the whole map of Europe will be changed.

Confucius Saw Nancy and Essays About Nothing, pp. 90–91

. . . there is never a human tragedy but has its comic elements. There was probably never an age when the practical affairs

68

of men did not look like a madhouse to some sane and perceptive minds, and there was never an age without its buffoons.

Between Tears and Laughter, p. 7

Slowly and laboriously has come the realization that the more we change, the more we remain the same; that underlying the superficial changes of government system, the essential state of things, the essential corruption, futility and incompetence remain, and the essential hopelessness.

My Country and My People, p. 350

It is in the very nature of things that good fortune and adversity alternate, that good and evil complement each other in life. All life is a mixture of the good and the bad. Everything moves in cycles. No nation is permanently strong. No family is permanently rich. No family is permanently powerful. No man remains in a position of permanent disadvantage. Human progress does not go forward in a straight line; it is not Heaven's way. History follows a zigzag course of progression and retrogression. Good and evil are often disguised phases of the same movement. Suffering and pain and slipbacks will always be with us. Just as the theory of evolution caused us to revise our concept of God's creation of man, so we must think of human progress as consisting in the movements of different forces, with advances and setbacks. It is through the alternation of cross currents, the struggle of dominant and recessive forces, that humanity will move ever forward and upward.

The Pleasures of a Nonconformist, pp. 65–66

No one realizes how beautiful it is to travel until he comes home and rests his head on his old, familiar pillow.

The Little Critic: Essays, Satires, and Sketches on China (Second Series: 1933–1935), p. 229

... the true motive of travel should be travel to become lost and unknown. More poetically, we may describe it as travel to forget. Everyone is quite respectable in his home town, no matter what the higher social circles think of him. He is tied by a set of conventions, rules, habits and duties. A banker finds it difficult to be treated just as an ordinary human being at home and to forget that he is a banker, and it seems to me, the real excuse for travel is that he shall be able to find himself in a community in which he is just an ordinary human being.

The Importance of Living, p. 331

A touch of sadness and a touch of madness make all the world akin. That is why we resent all great men who are presented to us without moral imperfections, without idiosyncrasies or some form of defect, mental or physical, like Cromwell's wart or President Wilson's hurting toes. There should be some personal weakness somewhere, or some intense love—a form of madness—be it for a woman or aeronautic science, a form of madness which implies absolute devotion to one thing and absent-mindedness or forgetfulness about all other things.

The Importance of Understanding, p. 18

The man who is overconscious of his nationality should not travel at all.

The Pleasures of a Nonconformist, pp. 182–183

smokers, but this nuisance is physical, while the nuisance that the non-smokers cause the smokers is spiritual.

The Importance of Living, p. 231

The task of adjustment between the old and the new is usually too much for the ordinary man. . . .

My Country and My People, p. 280

A palpable lie is praised if it is told in good form.

My Country and My People, p. 236

. . . all of us are full of contradictions just because we are human.

Confucius Saw Nancy and Essays About Nothing, p. 241

"Everybody exaggerates when he scores a point."

Looking Beyond, p. 234

I have lived long enough to know that no one can convince anybody by words unless he is convinced already anyway.

The Pleasures of a Nonconformist, p. 11

I am born naturally an honest man. When I disliked a man, I said so. When people criticized my point of view, I pointed out their errors. But one can't live in China for forty years without acquiring a little "fierceness." Now when I see my enemies, I smile. When people at table talk nonsense, I enjoy it, and do not

221

even object. . . . I ignore my critics and go on with my work and smile to everybody. I am very fierce. One of my friends whom I met at Hangchow a week ago remarked that Yutang has greatly improved, that in fact I am marvellous, that some day I shall be able to do great things.

The Little Critic: Essays, Satires and Sketches on China (Second Series: 1933–1935), pp. 122–123

Men resort to talking only when they haven't the power to enforce their convictions upon others.

The Importance of Living, p. 52

It is in the nature of things that a sham or a lie gets found out if the people are given enough time.

The Secret Name, p. 183

Anything is permissible so long as you call it by the wrong name.

My Country and My People, p. 237

There is never a time when a person wants to do a thing and fails to find reasons for his action, or when a great nation decides upon an objective and fails to find the plausible procedure. Sometimes to enter into argument with a person is to pay him the compliment of believing in the worth of his arguments.

Between Tears and Laughter, p. 39

. . . inconsistency is not a fault, but a virtue.

The Little Critic: Essays, Satires and Sketches on China (First Series: 1930–1932), p. 4

The world's best and worst resolutions are always made at the last moment.

The Little Critic: Essays, Satires and Sketches on China (Second Series: 1933–1935), p. 166

I have never been able to repeat Dr. Sun Yatsen's will, nor have I been able to keep my mind from wandering during the official three minutes of silent worship.

The Little Critic: Essays, Satires and Sketches on China (Second Series: 1933–1935), p. 190

A man who can sit all by himself at a club party and look damned comfortable is always imposing.

With Love and Irony, pp. 11–12

I have never been conscious of sin.

The Little Critic: Essays, Satires and Sketches on China (Second Series: 1933–1935), p. 193

Many men have circumvented sex, but no saint has yet circumvented food and drink.

The Importance of Living, pp. 43–44

"There are two classes of men as far as I am concerned; not economic classes, but classes of human beings: those that mind

223

their own business, and those who are not happy unless they mind that of others."

Looking Beyond, p. 218

The tragedy of the American spirit is that, when a fad does come about, so many applaud because they do not understand and so few laugh at them for telling them what they already know. There is already a tendency to talk of "the coefficient of happiness," and "secondary factors of social response in the tertiary stage of pattern-stimuli reaction in a general conformity drift in any highly industrialized social organization." God bless these idiots! These psychologists and sociologists are making life too complicated for us, as if modern life were not complicated enough already! Everybody is telling me that I may have within my being either an inflated or a deflated ego, a couple of reflex actions, three or four fixations, a perhaps not altogether too singular mother-love complex, a dozen inhibitions concealed somewhere in my psyche, in addition to some mild manifestation of sadistic impulse on some totally and apparently irrelevant lines. I have the libido, the eros, the id, which are all like squids as far as I am concerned, and now I may have a peculiarly high stimuli response and perhaps am in the category of all great business executives who by all intelligence tests show an alarmingly low I.Q.—lower than the average Columbia freshman. I must never say don't to my child for fear that I may establish an inhibition and be responsible for her persistent headaches forty years from now, and the child will grow up without inhibitions until he or she enters a business office and then at the age of twenty-two or twenty-three first learns that there are certain don'ts in life, the trangression of which neither life, nor God, nor society will condone.

On the Wisdom of America, pp. 52–53

It is astonishing how much one can accomplish by being regular.

The Pleasures of a Nonconformist, p. 117

. . . the one thing that a social upstart hasn't got and does not pretend to have is a sense of humor. Humor comes from self-confidence and taking things easy.

Confucius Saw Nancy and Essays About Nothing, p. 271

The building of the Great Wall was so efficient but so inhuman that it cost Tsin Shih Huang his empire.

The Pleasures of a Nonconformist, p. 111

All great men are humble. Su Tungpo was humble, in spite of his self-evident genius. One may find such among writers, but in politics, a truly humble great man is a rarity. What a difficult test for greatness!

The Importance of Understanding, p. 325

Snobs without money are vulgarians, and vulgarians with money are snobs.

The Importance of Understanding, p. 468

After all, a man can be quite a human being when he takes off his dog-collar and his stiff shirt, and comes home sprawling on the hearth-rug with a pipe in his hand.

The Little Critic: Essays, Satires and Sketches on China (Second Series: 1933–1935), p. iv

The modern man takes life far too seriously, and because he is too serious, the world is full of troubles.

The Importance of Living, p. 13

The most annoying moment in my life was when in the parlour of an American friend, a gigantic St. Bernard was trying to lick my hands and arms and be friendly, made worse by my hostess trying to tell me of his pedigree. I must have looked like a heathen at that time, staring at her blankly and not able to find an appropriate word of approval.

The Little Critic: Essays, Satires and Sketches on China (Second Series: 1933–1935), p. 241

Su Tungpo had charm. As with charm in women and beauty and fragrance in flowers, it is easier to feel it than to tell what elements it is composed of.

The Gay Genius, p. viii

I am usually not interested in people's morals.

Confucius Saw Nancy and Essays About Nothing, p. 92

The reason why man sometimes fails to realize the human best in him is because he has not come to a true understanding of the universe.

From Pagan to Christian, p. 82

. . . I am not qualified to be a bandit. Not only have I never killed a man (so far as I am directly aware of), but also I lack all

226

the admirable qualities which it takes to be a good bandit. A good bandit must be "a nice fellow" and have that divine inimitable sense of gay fellowship and camaraderie which I deplorably lack. A bandit chief must have all the necessary qualities of successful leadership, tact, knowledge of men, utter contempt of moral scruples, and, above all, a turncoat conscience. These are the qualities that I have noted in all successful leaders, and that I know I don't have.

The Little Critic: Essays, Satires and Sketches on China (First Series: 1930–1932), pp. 147–148

I don't mind sitting with either ambassadors or common people, but I can't stand ceremonious restraint and have no desire to impress people.

Quoted in Twentieth Century Authors, edited by Stanley J. Kunitz, p. 828

Effective planning of peace without a philosophy of peace is impossible. A revolution in thinking and in the method of thinking, of political events in particular and of human affairs in general, must be brought about before a revolution in world politics is possible.

Between Tears and Laughter, p. 58

Ultimately, there can be peace only when there is peace in the human heart; it cannot be imposed from without.

Between Tears and Laughter, p. 71

227

. . . truth can never be proved; it can only be hinted at.

My Country and My People, p. xiii

A holy cause is always a dangerous thing. When a cause becomes holy, the means used to achieve it inevitably becomes vile.

The Gay Genius, p. 5

Who ever said that Pontius Pilate was a bad man? He merely declined diplomatically to interfere in the private affairs of another nation, even though it involved the murder of an innocent man.

Between Tears and Laughter, p. 33

Mysticism usually frightens the people of a national temper chiefly because of the extravagances of some of its devotees.

The Wisdom of Laotse, p. 16

I have come to the conclusion that, in spite of the much touted technological development, the saving of a child's life, the return of a mother to him from Siberia, the liberating of one slave from his chains, is worth more than sending up those sputniks.

The Secret Name, p. 12

. . . let him cry whoever feels like crying, for we were animals before we became reasoning beings, and the shedding of a tear,

228

Who is really objective, and who can say that he alone is correct?

"The Educators' War About the Peace," Treasury for the Free World, edited by Ben Raeburn, 1946, p. 308

We have to have science, and we have to have elevators and escalators and hardwood floors and vacuum carpet-cleaners and fine galleries and museums and planetariums, and who but the dirty and philanthropic millionaire is going to endow your fine galleries and museums and planetariums? All the American research institutes and archeological museums represent a compromise between the spirit and the flesh, between science and ignoble capital.

Asia, November, 1936, p. 744

A more generous sympathy, or even tolerant cynicism, comes with a truer and deeper understanding of human nature which has its roots in our animal ancestry. Gently reminding ourselves that we are children of the Neanderthal or the Peking man, and further back still of the anthropoid apes, we eventually achieve the capacity of laughing at our sins and limitations, as well as admiring our monkey cleverness.

The Importance of Living, p. 33

Four thousand years of efficient living would ruin any nation.

The Importance of Living, p. 3

71

The most necessary outfit a traveler has to carry along with him is "a special talent in his breast and a special vision below his eyebrows," as the Chinese dramatic critic expressed it in his famous running comment on the drama *Western Chamber*. The point is whether one has got the heart to feel and the eyes to see. If he hasn't, his visits to the mountains are a pure waste of time and money; on the other hand, if he has got "a special talent in his breast and a special vision below his eyebrows," he can get the greatest joy of travel even without going to the mountains, by staying at home and watching and going about the field to watch a sailing cloud, or a dog, or a hedge, or a lonely tree.

The Importance of Living, p. 334

教育及文化

4

ON EDUCATION
AND
CULTURE

ΨΨΨ
ᛗᛗᛗ

The cultured man or the ideal educated man is not necessarily one who is well-read or learned, but one who likes and dislikes the right things. . . . An educated man, therefore, is one who has the right loves and hatreds.

The Importance of Living, pp. 362–363

It really does not matter at all to what college a man goes; the important thing is a good library. The quality of learning, like the kingdom of God, is within you, and it must come from the inside of your mind. The mind is a monkey; all you need to do is to let the monkey into a forest; you do not have to tell him where the nuts are to be found. You don't even have to guide him toward the good nuts.

From Pagan to Christian, p. 29

It is really extraordinary how we can all present a perfectly neat appearance at a friend's party, with shoes shined and tie to match (and the lady's handbag matching her shoes, too), and yet be disgracefully disorderly inside our heads.

On the Wisdom of America, p. 37

The wise man reads both books and life itself. The universe is one big book, and life is one big school.

The Importance of Living, p. 388

I am old-fashioned, and I do not feel the esthetic charm of artistic despair or of moral cynicism. I even like a little spanking in schools, which does no bodily harm but which most emphatically registers a sense of wrong and shame in a child's mind.

From Pagan to Christian, p. 220

We must give up the idea that a man's knowledge can be tested or measured in any form whatsoever.

The Importance of Living, p. 365

". . . one comes to maturity by breaking away from mere imitativeness."

Looking Beyond, p. 198

. . . educated ladies should not be a complete loss to society once they are married. . . .

The China Critic, November 20, 1930, p. 1143

In school and at college I always graduated second, because there was always some fool who took his classwork seriously, and who came out first.

From Pagan to Christian, p. 31

What one expects of a university graduate is not that he should become a learned scholar in his line, which is a flat impossibility in the four-year course, but that he should know his ropes, as we say, as far as his line is concerned, but far more important than that, that he should have an intelligent interest in the things of the mind, and should be able to think critically about the contemporary social, political and economic problems. That I take to be the mark of an educated man.

The China Critic, January 23, 1930, p. 79

Our conscious wisdom has nothing to do with our wisdom tooth.

The Importance of Living, p. 30

The more a teacher unsettles a man's smug, complacent notions and self-satisfactions, the greater usually is his unfluence.

From Pagan to Christian, p. 110

It is somewhat difficult to see character in a type of life where every man is throwing away his last year's car and trading it in for the new model.

The Importance of Living, pp. 164–165

Most minds continue to grow and mature by tossing about what one has learned from school and college.

From Pagan to Christian, p. 32

The love of good food, like the enjoyment of good music, is the unmistakable sign of culture.

The Pleasures of a Nonconformist, p. 123

77

LIN YUTANG: THE BEST OF AN OLD FRIEND

I have been told that an Oxford professor, one of those fine, broad minds which are the fruit of real culture, was one day upholding the Christian missionary movement in China from an entirely philosophic point of view. He showed how every nation profited from the introduction of foreign thoughts and ideals, how such an introduction could only be an enrichment and not an impoverishment of the nation's current of ideas in the long run, how Europe itself profited from the Greek and Roman heritage and England profited from the contact of continental thought. The professor had been talking, with great calmness and fine learning, for over twenty minutes, when his friend said, "But Rome and Greece did not send gun-boats to protect Homer and Horace and shoot the mediaeval Europeans whose souls Homer and Horace were trying to save." The professor saw the death of his arguments and buried them in a fit of amused, understanding laughter. The world would be an infinitely happier one to live in, if there were more such lightning flashes of wit and insight to clear the debris of academic wisdom.

The Little Critic: Essays, Satires and Sketches on China (Second Series: 1933–1935), pp. 167–168

It has been found in all countries and in all ages that, whenever there was a culture interested in the understanding of the art of living, there always developed a fashion of welcoming women in society.

The Importance of Living, p. 220

A natural man loves his children, but a cultured man loves his parents.

The Importance of Living, p. 193

The cultured Chinese . . . regards it as extremely bad form, as well as unwise, for a man to be over-assertive, or to push a fellow to the wall. That is called "not leaving ground for retreat," *pu liu yu ti*, for the opponent. And not to leave enough ground for retreat for the opponent indicates a real lack of culture, or *han-yang* as we call it.

The Pleasures of a Nonconformist, p. 113

The aim of education or culture is merely the development of good taste in knowledge and good form in conduct.

The Importance of Living, p. 362

. . . I am for amateurism in all fields. I like amateur philosophers, amateur poets, amateur photographers, amateur magicians, amateur architects who build their own houses, amateur musicians, amateur botanists and amateur aviators. I get as much pleasure out of listening to a friend playing a sonatina of an evening in an indifferent manner as out of listening to a firstclass professional concert.

The Importance of Living, pp. 366–367

Nothing is more exasperating than to meet a person at a party whose mind is crammed full with historical dates and figures and who is extremely well posted on current affairs in Russia or Czechoslovakia, but whose attitude or point of view is all wrong. I have met such persons, and found that there was no topic that might come up in the course of the conversation concerning which they did not have some facts or figures to produce, but whose points of view were deplorable. Such persons have erudition, but no discernment, or taste. Erudition is a mere matter of cramming of facts or information, while taste or discernment is a matter of artistic judgment.

The Importance of Living, p. 362

Modern philosophy of course has nothing to do with living, with the conduct of life. A modern college professor would be ashamed to say that he intends to teach right living. No, he teaches Greek thought, or medieval thought. We live in an age of fragmentizing of knowledge, of atomizing of knowledge. The synthesis of knowledge is not only lacking, but seems impossible. But the unifying of all knowledge used to be the business of philosophy.

The Pleasures of a Nonconformist, p. 101

The wisest man is often one who pretends to be a "damn fool."

The Importance of Living, p. 109

I am not convinced that all the idiots lived in the past and the great extraordinary minds live only in the present.

Between Tears and Laughter, p. 100

I want to be kind and sociable, but I want so much to say that a lot of modern psychology is often a study of the moron, for the moron, and by the moron that I might as well say it outright.

On the Wisdom of America, p. 51

The best way of studying any subject is to begin by reading books taking an unfavorable point of view with regard to it.

. . . After having read an author unfavorable to the subject, he is better prepared to read more favorable authors. That is how a critical mind can be developed.

The Importance of Living, p. 388

Determination of character, we are told, is a great virtue, but a qualification is necessary; so much depends upon what a man is determined to do.

The Gay Genius, p. 99

Modern specialization has gone so far that a specialist in bees has so much to find out about the bees that he has no time for the wasps.

The Pleasures of a Nonconformist, p. 83

I consider the education of our senses and our emotions rather more important than the education of our ideas.

The Importance of Living, p. 64

Business men who are busy the whole day and immediately go to bed after supper, snoring like cows, are not likely to contribute anything to culture.

The Importance of Living, p. 217

Scholars who are worth anything at all never know what is called "a hard grind" or what "bitter study" means. They merely love books and read on because they cannot help themselves.

The Importance of Living, p. 382

81

I admire the gentleman in America and feel sorry for him that he has to be ashamed of his culture and his better opinions—feel sorry that he has been cudgeled into conformity, caged in silence, and haunted by the fear of being different from the common man. I understand but nevertheless wonder at the fairly complete absence of gentlemen from politics.

With Love and Irony, pp. 27-28

Nothing is so soul-uplifting as to be assumed to understand a subject of which one has only hazy notions.

The Little Critic: Essays, Satires and Sketches on China (First Series: 1930-1932), p. 165

All my life, in China and abroad, I have been an enemy of the experts and a friend of simplification.

On the Wisdom of America, p. 425

You cannot improve the mental and moral qualities of men as easily as you increase the mileage of concrete highways or the speed of airplanes.

The Pleasures of a Nonconformist, p. 30

Maturity of spirit is the one quality of mind that, like wine, cannot be produced in a hurry. The breadth of spirit, the delight of insight, and the full and free luxuriant flowering of thought in writing, well conditioned, giving that stimulating sparkle and mellowed body in its draughts of thought, and satisfy-

82

ing our highest demands—these are the qualities which like wine, must mellow for decades in dark, cool, undisturbed cellars.

On the Wisdom of America, p. 239

In reading as in eating, what is one man's meat may be another's poison. A teacher cannot force his pupils to like what he likes in reading, and a parent cannot expect his children to have the same tastes as himself. And if the reader has no taste for what he reads, all the time is wasted.

The Importance of Living, p. 379

There are always wise souls who believe that the animals have a lot to teach us, and there are always open-minded persons who can see that man is the most degenerate of all animals and that a healthy return to original simplicity of character may be the salvation of mankind.

The Importance of Understanding, p. 346

There are in this world certain great teachers, whose personality seems to account for their influence more than their scholarship. We think of Socrates, or of St. Francis of Assisi, who themselves did not write any books of account, but who left such a tremendous impress on their generation that their influence persisted throughout the ages. The charm of Confucius was very much like the charm of Socrates; the very fact that the latter commanded the affection and respect of Plato is sufficient evidence of the power of his personality and his ideas.

The Wisdom of Confucius, p. 24

LIN YUTANG: THE BEST OF AN OLD FRIEND

One never learns anything from a book when he hates the author. Would that school teachers would bear this fact in mind!

The Importance of Living, p. 387

The pursuit of knowledge should remain nobody else's business but one's own, and only then can education become a pleasure and become positive.

The Importance of Living, p. 366

The process of education mainly consists in clearing oneself of a number of foolish presumptions, humbugs, and prejudices that beset the common man's mind. Some of the commonest assumptions and presumptions that are dangerous to a man's spiritual life are our worship of wealth and power and success, and beliefs in luck, adversity, and triumph over others, and the reality of the material world.

I Believe, pp. 169–170

It seems to me simplicity is about the most difficult thing to achieve in scholarship and writing. How difficult is clarity of thought, and yet it is only as thought becomes clear that simplicity is possible. When we see a writer belaboring an idea we may be sure that the idea is belaboring him. This is proved by the general fact that the lectures of a young college assistant instructor, freshly graduated with high honors, are generally abstruse and involved, and true simplicity of thought and ease of expression are to be found only in the words of the older professors. When a young professor does not talk in pedantic language, he is then positively brilliant, and much may be expected of him.

The Importance of Living, p. 81

84

The problem for any man intending to cultivate his personal life is merely to start out on a hunt for the best in his human nature and steadfastly to keep to it.

The Wisdom of Confucius, pp. 17–18

Culture is not something encased and embalmed. Culture is that free play of the mind, that perpetual dissatisfaction and refusal to accept the present as God-given. Culture is doubt. Much better is it to be torn by doubt and despair than to be smugly self-assured with a bowl of pottage. For of such stuff is culture made—the eternal capacity for self-improvement, with society as with individuals. To doubt, to dream, to stretch out one's arms and not fold them, to set out in eternal quest and to doubt one's own dream—these are the qualities that make for progress.

The Secret Name, p. 224

The need for today is for a humanizing of all knowledge that distributes relative importance and relates all values to the end of a happy human life. Modern knowledge has grown in incredible complexity; sooner or later it must return to simplicity again. It will need a simple viewpoint. Then we can afford to see the world go by. The world is like a market with many goods. What man can enjoy is what he brings home in his basket. Let us hope that he does not forget the basket, or bring an empty basket home.

The Pleasures of a Nonconformist, p. 106

I am one of these men who are always interested in trivialities.

Confucius Saw Nancy and Essays About Nothing, p. 74

All men and women have passions, natural desires and noble ambitions, and also a conscience; they have sex, hunger, fear, anger, and are subject to sickness, pain, suffering and death. Culture consists in bringing about the expression of these passions and desires in harmony.

The Importance of Living, p. 20

Culture, as I understand it, is essentially a product of leisure. The art of culture is therefore essentially the art of loafing. From the Chinese point of view, the man who is wisely idle is the most cultured man.

The Importance of Living, p. 150

The desire for success is killed by the shrewd hunch that the desire for success means very much the same thing as the fear of failure. The greater success a man has made, the more he fears a climb down. The illusive rewards of fame are pitched against the tremendous advantages of obscurity. From the Taoist point of view, an educated man is one who believes he has not succeeded when he has, but is not so sure he has failed when he fails, while the mark of the half-educated man is his assumptions that his outward successes and failures are absolute and real.

The Importance of Living, p. 161

. . . we have now come to a stage of human culture in which we have compartments of knowledge but not knowledge itself; specialization, but no integration; specialists but no philosophers of human wisdom. . . . Human wisdom cannot be merely the *adding up* of specialized knowledge or obtained by a study of statistical averages; it can be achieved only by insight, by the

86

general prevalance of more common sense, more wit and more plain, but subtle, intuition.

The Importance of Living, pp. 414–415

There is . . . a curious belief in some people that a proper accumulation of objective facts adds up to wisdom.

The Pleasures of a Nonconformist, p. 84

It is a truism to say that the culture of any nation is the product of its mind.

The Importance of Living, p. 3

To know what to love and what to hate is to have taste in knowledge.

The Importance of Living, p. 362

理智

5
ON
BEING
REASONABLE

The greatest ideal that man can aspire to is not to be a show-case of virtue, but just to be a genial, likable and reasonable *human being.*

The Importance of Living, p. 242

... humanism and the spirit of reasonableness are associated with the sense of humor and the sense of proportion, and rule out fanaticism of all sorts.

My Country and My People (rev. ed.), p. 421

The logical mind works with cut and dried distinctions. According to logic: If A is right, then B, which is opposed to A, is wrong. If you say to a Chinese, "A is right," he will say, "You are right." But if you say, "Perhaps B is right," the Chinese will say, "You are right." You say, "Evidently A and B cannot be both right. Mr. Lin, you are inconsistent." And the Chinese will say, "You are right."

The Pleasures of a Nonconformist, pp. 55–56

... nothing is so uninteresting as to spend one's life with a paragon of virtue as a husband or wife. I have no doubt that a

91

society of such perfectly rational beings would be perfectly fitted to survive, and yet I wonder whether survival on such terms is worth having. Have a society that is well-ordered, by all means— but not too well-ordered!

The Importance of Living, p. 59

If we were all completely rational beings, we should then, instead of growing into perfect wisdom, degenerate into automatons, the human mind serving merely to register certain impulses as unfailingly as a gas meter.

The Importance of Living, p. 59

In English, to be "reasonable" is often synonymous with "not to make exorbitant demands." To say to a man, "Do be reasonable" is the same as saying, "Make some allowance for human nature. Do not push a fellow too far." When Doolittle, the father of the flower girl in Pygmalion, wanted to touch Professor Higgins for a five-pound note, his appeal was, "Do be reasonable. If you are to have my daughter in your apartment, where do I come in as her father?" You see the reasonable appeal is always an appeal to human nature, in this case, to what his feelings should have been as the girl's father.

The Pleasures of a Nonconformist, p. 110

One has to submit to a certain amount of artificiality in life and be reasonable about it.

Confucius Saw Nancy and Essays About Nothing, p. 89

The party who admits being unreasonable is already defeated and condemned.

With Love and Irony, p. 35

Let us not always push things to their logical conclusions which is to kill them.

The Pleasures of a Nonconformist, p. 58

In the selection of husbands for my daughters, I shall have only one standard: is he a reasonable person? We cannot imagine perfect husbands and wives who never quarrel; we can only conceive of reasonable husbands and wives who quarrel reasonably and then patch up reasonably.

The Importance of Living, p. 422

When men are naturally reasonable and good-tempered and considerate, women do not suffer. Besides, women have always the weapon of sex, which they can use to great advantage. It is nature's guarantee for their equality.

My Country and My People, p. 147

The average mind . . . is charming rather than noble. Had the average mind been noble, we should be completely rational beings, without sins or weaknesses or misconduct, and what an insipid world that would be! We should be so much less charming as creatures. I am such a humanist that saints without sins don't interest me.

The Importance of Living, pp. 56–57

No one who is reasonable can be warlike; no one who is reasonable can be determined; no one who is reasonable can be a fanatic.

With Love and Irony, p. 35

93

As all animals obey their instincts for survival, they are all satisfied. What distinguishes men from animals is the rise of self-consciousness and reason.

On the Wisdom of America, p. 50

A reasonable man would always avoid fighting, if he could help it, and does not fight until he is hard pressed to it. He is more inclined to the exercise of that faculty for compromise, which sometimes can go so far as to dangerously approach cowardice in western eyes.

The Pleasures of a Nonconformist, p. 112

A reasonable reformer is not a new broom that will sweep the universe clean, but is always glad to leave some dirt behind. A reasonable teetotaller is an occasional winebibber; a reasonable anti-gambler is willing to play poker with five-cent stakes, and a reasonable vegetarian always relishes a roast Nanking duck or a blood-drippling beef-steak. As Confucius would have said, what boots it a man to have discovered the greatest scientific truth and be inhuman?

The Little Critic: Essays, Satires and Sketches on China (Second Series: 1933–1935), p. 126

Humanized thinking is just reasonable thinking. The logical man is always self-righteous and therefore inhuman and therefore wrong, while the reasonable man suspects that perhaps he is wrong and is therefore always right.

The Importance of Living, p. 423

Every touch of irrational behavior in a biography is a stroke in convincing reality.

The Importance of Living, p. 61

Run across any hall of honor, with statues of the great men of history lining the corridor, and you will perceive that rationality of conduct is probably the last thing to be recalled from their lives.

The Importance of Living, p. 60

When one cannot be powerful, one must choose to be dainty, and when one cannot be aggressive, one has to make a virtue of reasonableness.

My Country and My People, p. 26

I am ultra-modern. No one can accuse me of being conservative. I am not only for the Gregorian calendar, but am even for the thirteen-month calendar, in which all months have exactly four weeks or twenty-eight days. In other words, I am very scientific in my viewpoint and very logical in my reasoning.

The Little Critic: Essays, Satires and Sketches on China (Second Series: 1933–1935), p. 249

I think of the Spirit of Reasonableness as the highest and sanest ideal of human culture, and the reasonable man as the highest type of cultivated human being. . . . I look forward to the time when the people of the world will be informed with this reasonable spirit, both in their personal and their national affairs. Reasonable nations live in peace and reasonable husbands and wives live in happiness. . . . Only in a world of reasonable beings can we have peace and happiness. The Reasonable Age, if that should ever come about, will be the Age of Peace. It will be the age in which the Spirit of Reasonableness prevails.

The Importance of Living, pp. 421–422

The reasonable mind keeps a balance when the logical mind has lost it.

My Country and My People, p. 110

In saying that I have a common philosophy of life, therefore, I merely mean that, as an ordinary educated man, I have tried to adopt a reasonable and, as far as possible, harmonious attitude toward life, toward living, toward human society and the universe and God.

I Believe, p. 158

Much as I like reasonable persons, I hate completely rational beings.

The Importance of Living, p. 231

No philosophy, ancient or modern, dealing with the problems of human life has yet discovered a more profound truth than this doctrine of a well-ordered life lying somewhere between the two extremes—the Doctrine of the Half-and-Half. It is that spirit of sweet reasonableness, arriving at a perfect balance between action and inaction, shown in the ideal of a man living in half-fame and semi-obscurity; half-lazily active and half-actively lazy; not so poor that he cannot pay his rent, and not so rich that he doesn't have to work a little or couldn't wish to have slightly more to help his friends; who plays the piano, but only well enough for his most intimate friends to hear, and chiefly to please himself; who collects, but just enough to load his mantelpiece; who reads, but not too hard; learns a lot but does not become a specialist; writes, but has his correspondence to the *Times* half of the time rejected and half of the time published. . . .

The Importance of Living, p. 113

The ideal man is one who has tried honestly to do his best to live a decent life and to see the truth according to his lights. The ideal man for me is merely a reasonable man, willing to admit his mistakes and correct them. I don't ask for better creatures on this earth.

I Believe, p. 165

It is not plain that passion rather than reason rules the world?

The Importance of Living, p. 61

One can use reasonableness to settle a dispute but not to locate the relative positions of the heart and liver or determine the function of the pancreatic juice.

My Country and My People, p. 91

Any one who is reasonable, or who loves common sense, will avoid extremes.

*The Little Critic: Essays, Satires and Sketches on China
(First Series: 1930–1932),* p. 13

As in war and disputes, so in all normal intercourse, the essence of the reasonable spirit is a sort of "live and let live" philosophy, so well typified in Portia's appeal that justice be tempered with mercy.

The Pleasure of a Nonconformist, p. 113

The reasonable spirit humanizes all our thinking, and makes us less sure of our own correctness. Its tendency is to round out our ideas and tone down the angularities of our conduct. The opposite of the reasonable spirit is fanaticism and dogmatism of all sorts in thought and behavior, in our individual life, national life, marriage, religion and politics.

The Importance of Living, p. 424

"Let us be reasonable." This is an attitude of expecting neither too much nor too little. Man is, as it were, sandwiched between heaven and earth, between idealism and realism, between lofty thoughts and the baser passions. Being so sandwiched is the very essence of humanity; it is human to have thirst for knowledge and thirst for water, to love a good idea and a good dish of pork with bamboo shoots, and to admire a beautiful saying and a beautiful woman.

The Importance of Living, p. 21

I am always scared and ill at ease when I enter a house in which there are no ash trays. The room is apt to be too clean and orderly, the cushions are apt to be in their right places, and the people are apt to be correct and unemotional. And immediately I am put on my best behavior, which means the same thing as the most uncomfortable behavior.

The Importance of Living, pp. 231–232

The ideal world for mankind will not be a rational world, nor a perfect world in any sense, but a world in which imperfections are readily perceived and quarrels reasonably settled. For mankind, that is frankly the best we can hope for and the noblest dream that we can reasonably expect to come true. This seems to imply several things: a simplicity of thinking, a gaiety in philosophy and a subtle common sense, which will make this reasonable culture possible. Now it happens that subtle common sense, gaiety of philosophy and simplicity of thinking are characteristic of humor and must arise from it.

It is difficult to imagine this kind of a new world because our present world is so different. On the whole, our life is too complex, our scholarship too serious, our philosophy too somber, and our thoughts too involved. This seriousness and this involved complexity of our thought and scholarship make the present world such an unhappy one today.

The Importance of Living, pp. 80–81

友誼愛情及婚姻

6
ON FRIENDSHIP,
LOVE,
AND MARRIAGE

以

I am sure that the heart can shake a throne. It is the wholeness of love that accomplishes great things in this universe.

The Importance of Understanding, p. 118

. . . one knows only those whom one really understands, and one completely understands only those whom one really likes.

The Gay Genius, p. 1

If we admit that comfort is not a sin, then we must also admit that the more comfortably a man arranges himself in an armchair in a friend's drawing-room, the greater respect he is showing to his host. After all, to make oneself at home and look restful is only to help one's host or hostess succeed in the difficult art of hospitality. How many hostesses have feared and trembled for an evening party in which the guests are not willing to loosen up and just be themselves. I have always helped my hosts and hostesses by putting a leg up on top of a tea table or whatever happened to be the nearest object, and in that way forced everybody else to throw away the cloak of false dignity.

The Importance of Living, p. 209

103

Just as it is impossible for me to say whether I love my children physically or spiritually when I hear their chattering voices or when I see their plump legs, so I am totally unable to distinguish between the joys of the mind and the joys of the flesh. Does anybody ever love a woman spiritually without loving her physically?

The Importance of Living, p. 127

"We pay for what we love."

Looking Beyond, p. 217

An unmarried woman today suffers disadvantages in the present society that an unmarried man is exempt from. Only women who have gone forward to earn their own living know how unfair the present system is against them.

The Little Critic: Essays, Satires and Sketches on China (First Series: 1930–1932), p. 42

What is patriotism but love of the good things we ate in our childhood?

The Importance of Living, p. 46

No man who loves the trees truly can be cruel to animals or to his fellowmen.

The Importance of Living, p. 137

"Love of money often makes a man a coward, but love of power always makes a man a brute. It is the most degrading love of all. Love of material well-being seldom hurts others, but love of power and glory always does."

Looking Beyond, p. 243

For in civilization, however a man chafes and is angry at the robbers of our liberty, we are allowed only to express our sentiments by a light smile around our lips or at the tip of our pen. Our really impassioned tirades, in which we give full reins to our sentiments, may be heard only by a few of our most intimate friends. Hence the requisite condition of a true conversation is that we are able to air our views at leisure in the intimacy of a room with a few good friends and with no people around whom we hate to look at.

The Importance of Living, p. 213

If the old-fashioned marriage is a preposterously unfair deal for man, the free love union is going to be a preposterously unfair deal for woman. At least, until our social ethics change. For this reason, I believe in companionate marriage, in a marriage gone into with less feeling of a heroic leap into the dark, but with more thoughts for a true and permanent fellowship after a more sensible and more cautious experiment in the beginning.

The Little Critic: Essays, Satires and Sketches on China
(First Series: 1930–1932), pp. 58–59

The love of mankind which requires reasons is no true love.

The Importance of Living, p. 137

105

. . . where there is love for fellow men or interest in others, one senses it immediately. . . .

From Pagan to Christian, p. 234

The man with a pipe in his mouth is the man after my heart. He is more genial, more sociable, has more intimate indiscretions to reveal, and sometimes he is quite brilliant in conversation, and in any case, I have a feeling that he likes me as much as I like him.

The Importance of Living, p. 232

. . . life is harsh, and a man with a warm, generous and sentimental nature may be easily taken in by his cleverer fellowman. The generous in nature often make mistakes by their generosity, by their too generous regard of their enemies and faith in their friends. Sometimes the generous man comes home disillusioned to write a poem of bitterness.

The Importance of Living, p. 101

Anyone can run over the names of his friends and associates in his mind and verify this fact for himself, that those we like are not those we respect for distinguished ability and those we respect for distinguished ability are not those we like.

The Importance of Living, p. 110

Having no particular friend is having everybody as one's friend.

The Importance of Living, p. 332

106

Friends that meet at meals meet at peace. A good birds' nest soup or a delicious chow mein has the tendency to assuage the heat of our arguments and tone down the harshness of our conflicting points of view. Put two of the best friends together when they are hungry, and they will invariably end up in a quarrel. The effect of a good meal lasts not only a few hours, but for weeks and months. We rather hesitate to review unfavorably a book written by somebody who gave us a good dinner three or four months ago.

The Importance of Living, p. 44

Since human society began, with men getting together around campfires, or sitting on top of beer barrels with pipe in hand, or lounging in the leather chairs of a club room, that intercourse of spirits, that free and easy exchange and friction and sending back and forth of thoughts which is called a conversation, has always been one of the great pleasures of life.

On the Wisdom of America, p. 244

Really good friends don't write letters to each other, for in the complete trust of each other's friendship, no one needs to write. And after a few years of parting, they meet again and find the friendship as true as ever.

The Gay Genius, p. 60

. . . all life, particularly the domestic life, is a lesson in restraint.

The Importance of Living, p. 200

Verily I say unto you, those who seek romance in marriage shall lose it, and those who forget about romance and settle down to be just good, cheerful companions shall find it. For I warn you, the earlier you get rid of those foolish schoolgirl notions about love and romance, the better it is. For romance is going to disappear and in its place is going to be a more earthly, more realistic companionship of love and mutual respect.

> *Confucius Saw Nancy and Essays About Nothing*, pp. 229–230

. . . ideal husbands and wives and fathers and mothers are to be found in every age and country.

> *The Importance of Living*, p. 167

When a brilliant poet lives with a woman of plain common sense . . . it usually turns out that the wife rather than the husband shows superior wisdom. Always in marriage there is the continual play of the opposite and complementary forces of man and woman.

> *The Gay Genius*, pp. 59–60

The marriage system will be imperfect as long as human nature is imperfect.

> *My Country and My People*, p. 165

. . . no pipe smoker ever quarrels with his wife. The reason is perfectly plain: one cannot hold a pipe between one's teeth and at the same time shout at the top of one's voice. . . . When a wise wife sees her husband about to fly into a fit of rage, she should gently stick a pipe in his mouth and say, "There, forget about it!" This formula always works. A wife may fail, but a pipe never.

> *The Importance of Living*, pp. 232–233

108

"Many girls have plunged into the matrimonial sea without knowing the first rudiments of navigation."

Looking Beyond, p. 313

. . . marriage isn't just a matter of avoiding "burning," as St. Paul, the great bachelor, once suggested. It isn't always a question of "to marry" or "to burn." When a man is well past forty, it is often a question of to marry or to sit out in the cold.

*The Little Critic: Essays, Satires and Sketches on China
(First Series: 1930–1932)*, p. 49

We can speak or discuss business with almost any person, but there are very few people with whom we can truly hold a night's conversation. Hence, when we do find a true conversationalist, the pleasure is equal to, if not above, that of reading a delightful author, with the additional pleasure of hearing his voice and seeing his gestures.

The Importance of Living, pp. 211–212

One speaks of prostitutes as selling their sex, but it would be more proper and exact to speak of them as selling their bodies. Selling sex is a much more general affair. The mother who helps her débutante daughter to curl her hair before a ball in order to catch the eye of a young millionaire or English lord is as much selling her daughter's sex as the prostitute, and the department store manager who dismisses an old saleswoman to make place for a young, charming applicant is trying to sell her sex to his customers. Our common notion of morality is that it is highly moral for a woman to sell her sex for the benefit of her employer until her youth and beauty are ground out of her by the daily routine of standing eight hours on high heels, but it is immoral for a woman to sell her sex directly. . . .

The Little Critic: Essays, Satires and Sketches on China (Second Series: 1933–1935), pp. 185–186

. . . whenever men's morals relax it is the women who suffer, whether it be through divorce, concubinage, companionate marriage or free love. There is by nature something eternally unequal and unfair in the sexual arrangement. For sexual equality is an unknown word in nature, whose sole concern is the propagation of the race. The so-called modern marriages on a fifty-fifty basis have always become a seventy-five and twenty-five arrangement in favor of the man with the advent of children, and if the woman is sporting enough to release the husband "when love ceases" the man of forty enjoys advantages which the divorced woman of forty and mother of three children cannot have.

My Country and My People, p. 163

. . . the problem of being a good wife is principally the problem of finding a good husband, and conversely the problem of being a good husband is principally the problem of finding a good wife.

The Gay Genius, p. 158

Logically no man should get married, but practically all men should. . . .

My Country and My People, p. 111

110

You cannot blame man for having the sex instinct any more than you can blame the beaver for having it.

The Nation, May 6, 1939, p. 527

There is nothing so intimate in a man's life, or in a woman's, as marriage, nothing that goes so far toward leaving an imprint on the texture of life and on man's soul itself. Not even the love of a parent for his child, which certainly is the motive force of a good part of our lives and activities, goes quite so far in influencing one's character and the flavor and tone of living. It colors one's evenings at home, gives a personal atmosphere to one's garden, leaves an aroma in one's kitchen, cheers or depresses, soothes or wrecks one's nerves, and makes all the difference in the tremendous trifles of daily life—whether the jug of milk is warm, whether the coffee is hot at breakfast when the president of a corporation is going to meet his board of directors at ten that morning. "You are wrong there," I hear my reader say. "The president's wife has nothing to do with his breakfast nowadays." *"Tant pis,"* would be my reply. "Do you mean to say that the president of a corporation is no longer able to have the privilege which the farmer has, the knowledge that the scrambled egg is done not by a stranger, but by one he loves, even as his scrambled egg was prepared by his mother in his childhood?" If you take such a small daily disadvantage and add up all the small disadvantages of daily living that come from the loss of the intimate joy of association of two persons of different sex, life is hardly worth living.

On the Wisdom of America, p. 345

An old rogue is a man who has seen a lot of life, and who is materialistic, nonchalant, and skeptical of progress. At its best, this old roguery gives us mellowness and good temper, which in old men make many girls prefer them for husbands.

My Country and My People, p. 52

Buddhists have taught people to banish their sex desires by looking upon a beautiful young woman and reflecting that she is only a mass of fairly stable bones and not so stable flesh. One can fool oneself, but what ugly thoughts!

The Importance of Understanding, p. 477

. . . if we love a woman, we do not love her geometrical precision of features, but rather her ways and gestures in motion, her looks and smiles.

The Importance of Living, p. 159

112

政府及政權

7
ON GOVERNMENT
AND
POWER

Any man asked by a waitress whether he will have tea or coffee, with or without cream, cold or hot or iced, Ceylon tea or China tea, with lemon or milk, and one, two, or three lumps of sugar, knows that he is free.

On the Wisdom of America, p. 2

What a price nations have to pay for the ignorance of their leaders!

My Country and My People (rev. ed.), p. 406

The conviction has been steadily growing in my mind that the average Chinese government, and for that matter, many other governments, irrespective of political periods, has always had the largest collection of anemic, dyspeptic, and otherwise properly infected individuals, as compared with any other human organization, hospitals and asylums excluded, of course.

The Pleasures of a Nonconformist, p. 143

How completely the great problems of labor, unemployment and tariffs leave the mind of a defeated presidential candidate even two weeks after an election!

The Importance of Living, pp. 103–104

115

People who do not know how to talk against their government do not deserve a democracy. And the best government in the world, when it is deprived of the goading of democratic "gadflies," soon gets bored with its own virtues and dies of inanity. I sometimes think God Himself created Satan because He was so sick of the singing and flattering angels and wanted to save Himself from boredom. If the kingdom of heaven cannot do without opposition, how much less can a human secular government? . . . Ability to talk against the government is an indication of adult democratic citizenship.

The Vigil of a Nation, pp. 213–214, 217

I think every nation eventually gets the kind of government that it deserves.

The China Critic, March 27, 1930, p. 296

I have such a strong dislike of petty politicians that I have never been able to carry on a fight with them in any organization that I am connected with. I have always run away to avoid seeing them, for I don't like their faces.

The Little Critic: Essays, Satires and Sketches on China (Second Series: 1933–1935), pp. 192–193

Alas, our rulers are not gods, but puny, fallible men, like the kings who constantly forget their parts, and we common men should be their prompters.

Between Tears and Laughter, p. 7

. . . the rules of politics are similar enough in the East and West. It is a system designed to ensure the rise of mediocrity to the top. There are certain rules of the game, played chiefly behind

116

the scenes. The first rule is, a good politician is one who has mastered the art of saying nothing with a great number of words. A good official never states, but only denies. With a sufficient schooling in the art of saying perpetually, "No comment," and "You are right," a good official can go a long way. A second rule is that he should oblige his friends. A third rule is that he should take care not to offend. With a tight mouth, a cultivated, low, pleasant whisper, and a great desire to oblige, such a man can never be thrown out of power even if he does not rise to the top. He will die at his desk.

The Gay Genius, p. 287

It really seems that a man can do much more for his country when he is serving on the land than at the capital.

The Gay Genius, p. 301

Student movements, abnormal in peaceful times, are nevertheless entirely normal in times of national distress. When there is a free press and a comparatively free outlet for public opinion, say through a House of Parliament, the student movements do not grow into any magnitude or importance, as is the case in the history of England. But when a government is faced with a situation which it cannot handle satisfactorily in the opinion of the people and normal outlets are denied, student movements must be regarded as entirely natural phenomena. Equally natural is the attitude of the government in trying to suppress it, for governments in the world seldom admit to themselves the truth that they really do not know how to govern, or that they are incapable of finding solutions to problems that are too big for the average human mind.

A History of the Press and Public Opinion in China, p. 46

. . . politics is the dark side of anything; it is the seat bottom of any people's culture.

Between Tears and Laughter, p. 93

I have always liked a revolution, but have never liked the revolutionists.

*The Little Critic: Essays, Satires and Sketches on China
(Second Series: 1933–1935),* p. 192

Even with the facilities of a free press, it always takes considerable time for the public to catch up to what the government is doing or not doing.

Between Tears and Laughter, p. 101

The idea of government by virtue and by benevolent rulers is just as fantastic to contemplate as the idea of motor traffic regulation on Broadway by the spontaneous courtesy of drivers instead of by a system of red and green lights.

Harpers Magazine, May 1935, p. 726

The reason I don't like dictators is that they are inhuman, and anything which is inhuman is bad. An inhuman religion is no religion, inhuman politics is foolish politics, inhuman art is just bad art, and the inhuman way of life is the beast's way of life.

The Importance of Living, p. 242

118

We must realize . . . that all speech is a nuisance and that the liberty of speech is still a greater nuisance in the eyes of the officials. The officials like quiet people who do not talk and who do not squeal when hurt. For instance, if there is a detective of the Public Safety Bureau here among you, I am sure he is thinking me a great nuisance, while he thinks all of you who sit there so quietly and "keep your mouths shut like vases" are better citizens than myself. This lies in the nature of things. You must realize that the liberty of speech we demand for the people means that there is going to be no liberty of action for the officials. The officials love their liberty as much as we love ours. When you demand liberty of the press, you are really demanding that the officials' liberty to muzzle the press be taken away from them. When you demand liberty of person as a constitutional right, you are taking away from the officials their liberty to chop off people's heads.

The Little Critic: Essays, Satires and Sketches on China (Second Series: 1933–1935), p. 146

After long hours of philosophizing, I am now willing to make the brave and hard admission that women are just human beings like men—equal in ability to make judgments and mistakes, if you give them the same world experience and contacts; in ability to do efficient work and keep a cool head, if you give them the same business training; in social outlook, if you don't shut them up in the home; and finally, in the capacity to rule and misrule, for if women should rule the world, they couldn't possibly make a greater mess of it than men have. . . .

With Love and Irony, p. 19

119

. . . by democracy I mean that of Will Rogers; for he is to me the most typical American, with his hatred of the dress suit and the white tie and all forms of snobbery and his cheerful, carefree humor. The democracy of Will Rogers is worth having.

Asia, November, 1936, p. 745

All governments tend to act like children at times, and they benefit from having a free press to call their folly.

The Vigil of a Nation, p. 215

I have never written a line that pleased the authorities or secured their admiration, nor have I been able to draft a single pronunciamento that has met with the approval of the great men.

The Little Critic: Essays, Satires and Sketches on China (Second Series: 1933–1935), p. 191

Modern democracy with universal suffrage is based upon the judgment of the common man, who often cannot follow a *New York Times* editorial.

The Gay Genius, p. 258

The ultimate test of any democracy is how far the people's opinions are able to influence or actually direct and control the policies of its government.

A History of the Press and Public Opinion in China, p. 115

Complete confidence in one's rulers would ruin any democracy.

The Pleasures of a Nonconformist, p. 36

It is true that freedom of the press is a nuisance for the rulers, but the difference between Fascists or Communists and believers in democracy is that, while the Fascists regard the press as a nuisance and therefore suppress it, the believers in democracy also regard the freedom of the press as a nuisance and thank God they have such a glorious nuisance. The press, the Congress, and in fact all democratic institutions are, or are intended to be, nuisances to the rulers.

Asia, November, 1936, p. 745

The fathers of the American Republic bet on democracy as one would bet on a horse.

On the Wisdom of America, p. 177

There is always a latent hostility between the ruler and the ruled, for government, under whatever form—whether it be democracy or limited or absolute monarchy—is always a tug-of-war between the ruler and the people: if the government wins, the people must lose, and if the government loses, the people must win. If this were not so, democracy, with all its claptrap of paraphernalia for hampering the freedom and shackling the authority of officials, would have no reason for existence at all.

A History of the Press and Public Opinion in China, p. 2

I have never been cool and detached and unimpassioned and diplomatic in discussing my country's politics. I have never been scholarly and weak-kneed and hypocritical.

The Little Critic: Essays, Satires and Sketches on China (Second Series: 1933-1935), p. 193

121

I am about to witness the presidential election, a kind of brain fever which catches the American nation once every four years, as regularly as malaria. I am going to see who can tell the biggest lie to the people, Republican or Democrat. If the greatest liar is a Republican, they are going to have a Republican President, and if the greatest liar is a Democrat, they are going to have a Democratic President. I am speaking of the party machinery and not of the presidential candidates personally, for a presidential candidate is merely an honest man sent around the country to lie on behalf of his party.

Asia,, November, 1936, p. 745

. . . it is terribly serious when our rulers do not smile, because they have got all the guns.

The Importance of Living, p. 78

. . . human nature is still the same, whether man lives in a socialist or capitalist state. Utopias where everybody loves and trusts everybody else do not come that easy.

From Pagan to Christian, p. 77

I like Americans best when I see them breaking laws and regulations, when I see at a movie theater that the audience's sympathy is with the stowaway and not with the law-upholding captain, and when I see on the trains between Washington and New York people smoking in every car marked "No Smoking." These are born democrats, I say. When the situation gets bad enough, it is not the Herr Conductor that will stop it, but the public, by somebody writing to the *New York Times* pleading against the danger of ashes burning babies' arms. If the public does not mind, neither will the American conductor. But imagine

122

a Prussian crowd smoking in a car where smoking is *verboten!* They just can't do it, and that is why the Weimar Republic fell and the *Frankfurter Zeitung* turned tail and they needed a Hitler. Put a Hitler over an American crowd to tell them not to do this and not to do that, and see the result. He would not survive three months before his head was smashed. Democracy's reply to Prohibition was the speakeasies. The history of the speakeasies is the glorious history of exactly how much the American people would stand for *verbotens,* and of how they would obey even laws passed by themselves!

Between Tears and Laughter, p. 67

The whole progress of democracy is based on an uncanny distrust and suspicion that its rulers, if left alone, would tend to abuse their powers.

The Pleasures of a Nonconformist, p. 36

The logic of history teaches us that whenever a man can commit enough murders on a national scale, he is always rewarded by a wave of public tributes.

A History of the Press and Public Opinion in China, p. 72

. . . if horses could talk to their jockeys, there could be no races at all. Horses must be whipped to victory, at least so think the jockeys and the Mussolinis and Hitlers of the world. Anyone who maintains his belief in democratic government, or a parliament or a public press, is only saying that the horses should talk to their jockeys and now and then question their motives and wisdom.

A History of the Press and Public Opinion in China, p. 3

123

I hate censors and all agencies and forms of government that try to control our thought. I cannot but believe that such a censor or such a ruler is wilfully or unintentionally insulting human intelligence. If the liberty of thought is the highest activity of the human mind, then the suppression of that liberty must be the most degrading to us as human beings.

The Importance of Living, pp. 71–72

... there is a growing tendency to hand over the government of the country to bureaucrats and "experts," and the terms on which the people are told to surrender their judgment to them are that these experts have "all the facts," which the people, the poor laymen, are not supposed to have. This is perhaps natural in view of the growing complexity of modern problems, but it also means that we are losing faith in the common man—an unhealthy, undemocratic tendency. . . . Remember only one thing: the experts have all the facts, while the people have all the judgment. This faith must not be shaken, for when it is shaken, democracy falls into the hands of the experts, and when democracy falls into the hands of the experts, democracy just falls.

Between Tears and Laughter, pp. 95, 98

One cannot win a war for democracy by dictatorial methods.

Between Tears and Laughter, p. 85

Perhaps electioneering apparatus is the necessary evil of an organized democracy, though I despise it. Every time I watch an election campaign in America, I lose faith in democracy. It has got to be done. But the spirit of democracy resides elsewhere. It resides in the spirit of free men who in their daily lives practice the unwritten law of democratic citizens who cannot be taken advantage of by others. It resides in the spirit of men who breathe the air of freedom in thinking and belief, and tolerate others' thinking and beliefs, and somehow by faith in the essential decency of human nature can get a government going for the common good.

The Vigil of a Nation, pp. 221–222

. . . I was by nature born into the class to be ruled by others, who send me questionnaires to be answered.

The Vigil of a Nation, p. 212

The Confucian system assumes every ruler to be a gentleman, and proceeds to treat him as a gentleman. The legalist system assumes every ruler to be a crook and proceeds to make provisions in the political system to prevent him from carrying out his crooked intentions.

*The Little Critic: Essays, Satires and Sketches on China
(First Series: 1930–1932)*, p. 64

. . . many wise men know that the desires for success, fame and wealth are euphemistic names for the fears of failure, poverty and obscurity, and that these fears dominate our lives. There are many people who have already attained both fame and wealth, but who still insist on ruling others. They are the people who have consecrated their lives to the service of their country. The price is often very heavy. Ask a wise man to wave his silk hat to a crowd and make seven speeches a day and give him a presidency, and he will refuse to serve his country.

I think the strenuousness of a presidential campaign alone

125

is enough to frighten off all the wise souls of America. A public office often demands that a man attend six dinners a week in the name of consecrating his life to the service of mankind. Why does he not consecrate himself to a simple supper at home and to his bed and his pyjamas?

The Importance of Living, p. 103

. . . we must ask whether a poet-painter can become a successful official. Conceivably, yes, in time of peace, but peace is a relative word, and there is not a decade in politics in which there are not hot issues to fight about. A poet-painter, with his detached philosophic point of view, can scarcely become so involved in the political issues that he is willing to play the game and accept the penalties. More often than not, after a few trials, he laughs at himself for trying to play it at all.

The Gay Genius, p. 287

"When a man begins to believe himself a demigod, he becomes a danger to mankind."

Looking Beyond, p. 243

Real dignity in government comes from taking leadership of the nation and giving effective expression to the will of the people, and not by going against it and then taking the choice of suppressing public criticism or being forced into line with it.

A History of the Press and Public Opinion in China, p. 53

The common man is the rock of American democracy because he, rather than the gentleman, represents the greatest num-

126

ber, to whom the greatest numbers of things are to be sold, and for whom radio programs and movies are being made—and what is American democracy if the manufacturers don't sell products by the hundreds of thousands and make movies for the millions?

With Love and Irony, p. 21

When it is too dangerous for a man to be public-spirited, it is natural that he should take an apathetic attitude toward the country, and when there is no punishment for greedy and corrupt officials, it is too much to ask of human nature to ask them not to be corrupt.

The Little Critic: Essays, Satires and Sketches on China (First Series: 1930–1932), p. 69

Democracy is a system of government based on the association of men who believe that peace, security, and justice for all can somehow be worked out by a delegation of their powers to freely elected bodies, provided the people can at any time peacefully throw out any government that doesn't give them peace, security, and justice.

The Vigil of a Nation, pp. 211–212

The Chinese government, like all western governments, always thinks that it is capable of handling the situation if left alone, and resents criticism from the outside while the Chinese people, again like all the people in the world, persist in thinking the government of the time the worst one they could possibly have. The government always claims that it is thinking of the people, but does not quite like to hear what the people think of itself. What the government really wants is that the people should stop thinking altogether—a dumb, unthinking herd that takes orders unquestioningly and can be driven into the pastures or the slaughter-house at its own sweet will.

A History of the Press and Public Opinion in China, p. 3

He who has the heaviest tanks and thickest prison walls but has lost the hearts of men under him is not to be feared. To put it more explicitly, I firmly believe that it is against the dictum of all human history that human enslavement can last forever. He who must suppress the human cry for freedom by secret police methods is already lost. For that is the verdict of history, and it is the verdict of history because among the many instincts of men, there is not an instinct for slavery.

The Secret Name, p. 14

Democracy is a hard thing to learn both for the rulers and for the ruled. In its essence, it implies the ability of the majority to rule and the ability of the minority to criticize and abide by the majority. Even in a small group of boys playing in the streets or three office girls sharing one apartment, democracy means no more than these simple habits of thinking. When the ruling party forgets that it is only elected to rule by the rest of the group and tends to suppress criticism of its actions, it is to that extent undemocratic. When the minority group fails to abide by the majority and prefers to break away and form a separate gang, it, too, becomes undemocratic.

The Vigil of a Nation, p. 222

. . . there is not very much difference in actual happiness between living a luxurious life and a simple one. The honor of a high position appears enviable only to one who is unqualified for it. The usual rule is, one is wanted for a post when he does not want it, and one wants a post when the post does not want him. Once the "official craving" is satisfied, being a high official is not likely to be more fun than being a successful blacksmith.

The Gay Genius, p. 266

For leadership in a democracy always consists in marking time and being pushed by the people from behind. There the great leader stands, with a glad eye cast on the right and a twinkling eye on the left, while he marks time with his steps. If he is pushed hard enough from the right, he totters to the left, and if he is pushed hard enough from the left, he totters to the right. Only thus is he able to lead the people. And if he is successfully pushed in the direction we want him to go, we acclaim him a "great man." That is why I love democracy, for I enjoy pushing around our leaders, and why I detest tyrants, for I resent being pushed around.

Between Tears and Laughter, p. 100

A nation is a concern, a government is only its shop counter, and its diplomats are its traveling salesmen trying to outsell its competitors and beat them to a new market, and its publicists and thinkers are its expert accountants.

Between Tears and Laughter, p. 62

Democracy after all simply means that the average man can and will take an intelligent interest in man's group life. . . .

A History of the Press and Public Opinion in China, p. 179

Democracy itself is predicated upon the principle of disagreement among parties.

The Gay Genius, p. 119

"All socialistic experiments have failed; some were never meant to be put into practice. Plato's community of wives and children, his eugenics and his philosopher-king. His *Republic* was an inquiry written down for his own pleasure as to what an ideal country should be; I don't think he ever entertained the idea of seeing his *Republic* brought into existence."

Looking Beyond, p. 47

A soldier's duty is but to do and die; a good politician's is just to do and never talk about it.

From Pagan to Christian, p. 43

Of course, socialism is an absurdity, when it not only permits, but encourages inequality of income. Of course a democracy which is a totalitarian state is an absurdity. Of course an election which is a race with one horse is an absurdity.

The Secret Name, p. 10

Who sins against unity in time of war sins against the nation as a whole.

The Vigil of a Nation, p. 126

Civil wars are necessary in a nation until an equilibrium is restored.

Between Tears and Laughter, p. 145

思想

8
ON
THE ART OF
THINKING

゛゛゛
ፚፚ

May I walk around hell free and alone rather than be led around heaven in chains!

On the Wisdom of America, p. 169

. . . I do not justify my likes and dislikes. Personal likes and dislikes are things that you do not have to give reasons for. They are just personal likes and dislikes. I like certain things because I like them. To every question about the reason for my preferences, the answer is, "Just because."

With Love and Irony, p. 24

There is in this life no argument quite as effective as somebody being able to take away your bread from your mouth.

The Secret Name, p. 114

I have never cared which way the wind blows.

The Nation, March 24, 1945, p. 324

Censors the world over always occupy a ridiculous position. In whatever country and age, few censors have succeeded

135

in avoiding making themselves alternately cursed and laughed at.

A History of the Press and Public Opinion in China, p. 167

A man who exercises common sense is like a whale who every so many minutes must come up to the surface to breathe and take a glance at the sea and the skies around. The logical thinker is like a man who dives to the bottom of the sea and feels no need to come up again.

The Pleasures of a Nonconformist, p. 53

A lecture without an audience gives you a lot of liberty.

Confucius Saw Nancy and Essays About Nothing, p. 227

I believe women think and feel on the whole very much as men do, that mentally there is much less sex difference than physically, although some women like to encourage the men to think otherwise.

On the Wisdom of America, p. 68

"There ought to be a law requiring a professor of philosophy to explain his thoughts to his maidservant. If he cannot do that, he ought to be disqualified, disfranchised, summarily dismissed."

Looking Beyond, p. 229

"Only stagnant water stinks, fresh water doesn't, and . . . dogmatism is the stagnation of the mind. It means the mind has shut up, refuses to do more thinking."

Looking Beyond, p. 89

It is better to leave off without a conclusion than to have a bad conclusion.

The Pleasures of a Nonconformist, p. 121

. . . it should be remembered that unless censorship is intelligent, it is worse than useless and often defeats its own ends.

A History of the Press and Public Opinion in China, p. 175

Clear thoughts expressed in unclear language is the style of a confirmed bachelor. He never has to explain anything to a wife.

The Importance of Living, p. 387

All . . . of us are merely repeating what others have thought, though many have made their own discoveries by some thinking of their own. By "original minds" I mean the thinkers who broke unknown grounds for human thought, whose thinking soared to heights where others had not been before.

From Pagan to Christian, p. 174

. . . it is not our surroundings, but our reactions toward them that count.

The Importance of Living, p. 90

It is important that man dreams, but it is perhaps equally important that he can laugh at his own dreams.

The Importance of Living, pp. 4–5

Laotse says, "Nature does not talk," nor does the old pine tree. There it stands silent and imperturbable; from its height it looks down upon us, thinking it has seen so many children grow up into maturity and so many middle-aged people pass on to old age. Like wise, old men, it understands everything, but it does not talk, and therein lie its mystery and grandeur.

The Importance of Living, p. 299

A thing may sound so logical you are convinced it must be wrong. The moment a philosophical system becomes too impressive or logically beautiful, I become suspicious.

I Believe, p. 157

Man does not talk because he thinks, but thinks because he talks, because he has words to play with, and thinking is only the tumbling about of words.

From Pagan to Christian, pp. 58–59

No one begins to think until he has some of that brute complacency thoroughly thrashed out of him with the rawhide of the wiser minds.

On the Wisdom of America, p. xii

. . . when any one announces that he is going to speak his mind freely, every one is frightened. This shows that there is no such thing as true freedom of speech. No one can afford to let his neighbours know what he is thinking about them. Society can exist only on the basis that there is some amount of polished lying and that no one says exactly what he thinks.

The Little Critic: Essays Satires and Sketches on China (Second Series: 1933–1935), p. 143

Freedom of belief means you can believe anything you like, provided you don't at the same time use the freedom of speech to let others know what you believe.

On the Wisdom of America, p. 309

Blessed is the man who knows a thing is so without being able to explain why it is so.

The Pleasures of a Nonconformist, p. 53

. . . who are we anyway to be censors of other people's thoughts and ideas?

A History of the Press and Public Opinion on China, p. 167

The free world can survive with honest-thinking men, not with politicians.

The Secret Name, p. 185

Women have a more robust common sense than men, and in times of any emergency, I always depend on the judgment of a woman rather than that of a man. They have a way of sizing up a situation in its totality without being distracted by its individual aspects.

My Country and My People, p. 90

139

I have not called the moon square one day and called it round a week afterwards, for I have a very strong memory.

*The Little Critic: Essays, Satires and Sketches on China
(Second Series: 1933–1935)*, p. 191

To me wisdom and courage are the same thing, for courage is born of an understanding of life; he who completely understands life is always brave. Anyway that type of wisdom which does not give us courage is not worth having at all. Wisdom leads to courage by exercising a veto against our foolish ambitions and emancipating us from the fashionable humbug of this world, whether humbug of thought or humbug of life.

The Importance of Living, p. 102

Anybody who wants to champion the people's right of speech must have eunuchs for his enemies.

*The Little Critic: Essays, Satires and Sketches on China
(Second Series: 1933–1935)*, p. 148

There is no greater robber in this world than he who robs us of our liberty of thought. Deprived of that, we might as well go down on all fours, call the whole biped experiment of walking on two legs a mistake, and revert to our earlier posture of at least some 30,000 years ago.

The Importance of Living, p. 72

Oh, how I love to reach home by climbing over the back fence, and to travel on bypaths!

The Importance of Living, pp. vii-viii

The dissenter, the man who refuses to conform, is still the man for me.

The Pleasures of a Nonconformist, p. 23

All thoughts come in flashes. They should stand by themselves. When they are expanded, they lose some of the force of the original thoughts.

The Importance of Understanding, p. 461

. . . I can write only of my own perceptions and insights and my own evaluations and interpretations.

From Pagan to Christian, p. 67–68

I fail to see why westerners always personify "Liberty," "Victory," "Peace" or "Justice" in the form of either a half-draped or a completely naked woman. Why can't these lofty and noble sentiments be represented by the male sex instead?

The Little Critic: Essays, Satires and Sketches on China (Second Series: 1933–1935), p. 73

The greater the imaginative power of a man, the more perpetually he is dissatisfied.

The Importance of Living, p. 74

The most constant refrain of our thought occurring unfailingly every few hours is, "When do I eat?"

The Importance of Living, p. 44

. . . man is yet incapable of thinking internationally, nor do I think he ever will be.

The Little Critic: Essays, Satires and Sketches on China (Second Series: 1933–1935), p. 32

The fonder you are of your ideals, the greater your heartbreaks.

Between Tears and Laughter, p. 6

When a person is hungry, he has very decided opinions, and the same is true of nations as of individuals.

A History of the Press and Public Opinion in China, p. 4

Let those who like to indulge in pontifical truths and professorial formulas have them; let me have the colors and sounds and smells. Thus it may be found that I am more concerned in recording the little things on the avenue of life, as they seemed to me and as I felt them.

The Vigil of a Nation, p. 6

I do not know what the world thinks of fishermen and I do not care.

The Pleasures of a Nonconformist, p. 19

He who preaches any kind of doctrine must be prepared to be misunderstood.

The Importance of Living, p. 137

I will let others keep their opinions if I am allowed to keep mine.

The Pleasures of a Nonconformist, p. 11

A committee meeting provides a great chance for some people who like to hear their own voices to talk and talk, while others draw crocodiles or a lady's legs. It also prevents the men who can think and make quick decisions from doing so.

The Pleasures of a Nonconformist pp. 32–33

Better to have come to no conclusions than not to have wondered at all.

From Pagan to Christian, p. 111

Constant forgettings of truths once perceived are the very charm of the human mind; the history of human thought is nothing more than the story of these forgettings and rememberings and forgettings again.

On the Wisdom of America, p. xiv

Our international world is rapidly coming to the end of an era. So is our modern intellectual world. The world of ideas is definitely going to pieces, because our traditional values are gone.

The Wisdom of China and India, p. 570

Thinking, real thinking, is granted to only a few individuals, and to others only at moments of clear and unbiased vision. Our opinions and beliefs are coloured by social, religious and race prejudices, and are often influenced by our full-mouthed orators, journalists and propagandists.

The China Critic, January 23, 1930, p. 81

As in a democracy, the sovereignty derives ultimately from the individual voter, so in the realm of thinking, the individual is his own authority. . . . We all submit to social conventions, contribute to charities, read the current popular books, and go to church. But at least in the realm of thought, man ought to reassert his independence. The mind always dares in the solitude of one's study in the still hours of the night. In such thinking, there is strength. In such nonconformity he asserts his rights as a man: "Whoso would be a man must be a nonconformist."

The Pleasures of a Nonconformist, pp. 17–18

There is a method of appealing to one's own intuitive judgment, of thinking out one's own ideas and forming one's own independent judgments, and confessing them in public with a childish impudence, and sure enough, some kindred souls in another corner of the world will agree with you. A person forming his ideas in this manner will often be astounded to discover how another writer said exactly the same things and felt exactly the same way, but perhaps expressed the ideas more easily and more gracefully. It is then that he discovers the ancient author and the ancient author bears him witness, and they become forever friends in spirit.

The Importance of Living, p. ix

. . . to have taste or discernment requires a capacity for thinking things through to the bottom, and independence of

144

judgment, and an unwillingness to be bulldozed by any form of humbug, social, political, literary, artistic, or academic.

The Importance of Living, p. 363

A "scholar's" writing consists of borrowings from other scholars, and the more authorities and sources he quotes, the more of a "scholar" he appears. A thinker's writing consists of borrowings from ideas in his own intestines, and the greater thinker a man is, the more he depends on his own intestinal juice.

The Importance of Living, pp. 388–389

No one need be afraid of the harvest of his opinions; no writer should be afraid if they are his own.

The Pleasures of a Nonconformist, p. 11

Too much thinking will bring about mankind's destruction.

Confucius Saw Nancy and Essays About Nothing, p. 100

I rather despise claims to objectivity in philosophy; the point of view is the thing.

The Importance of Living, p. vii

Let every man have the courage to think for himself. In this capacity of man to think for himself . . . lies the true motive force of all human progress.

The Pleasures of a Nonconformist, p. 27

Now it must be taken for granted that simplicity of life and thought is the highest and sanest ideal for civilization and culture, that when a civilization loses simplicity and the sophisticated do

145

not return to unsophistication, civilization becomes increasingly full of troubles and degenerates. Man then becomes the slave of the ideas, thoughts, ambitions and social systems that are his own product. Mankind, overburdened with this load of ideas and ambitions and social systems, seems unable to rise above them. Luckily, however, there is a power of the human mind which can transcend all these ideas, thoughts and ambitions and treat them with a smile, and this power is the subtlety of the humorist. Humorists handle thoughts and ideas as golf or billiard champions handle their balls, or as cowboy champions handle their lariats. There is an ease, a sureness, a lightness of touch, that comes from mastery. After all, only he who handles his ideas lightly is master of his ideas, and only he who is master of his ideas is not enslaved by them. Seriousness, after all, is only a sign of effort, and effort is a sign of imperfect mastery. A serious writer is awkward and ill at ease in the realm of ideas as a *nouveau riche* is awkward, ill at ease and self-conscious in society. He is serious because he has not come to feel at home with his ideas.

The Importance of Living, p. 81

For the world is both a good and a bad world, and man is both a noble and a wicked creature. Life is often so happy and often so sad, and human society is often so cruel, and yet often not lacking in true kindness. Knowing that this is the case, how shall we proceed except by eminently kind, tolerant, and ironic thinking? Great wisdom consists in not demanding too much of human nature, and yet not altogether spoiling it by indulgence. One must try to do one's best, and at the same time, one must, when rewarded by partial success or confronted by partial failure, say to himself, 'I have done my best.' That is about all the philosophy of living that one needs.

I Believe, pp. 159–160

146

文學

及藝術

9
ON
LITERATURE
AND ART

Writing, writing, writing! What is writing compared with life?

The Little Critic: Essays, Satires and Sketches on China (Second Series: 1933–1935), p. 194

A great work of art requires a finely appreciative soul to draw from it the full enjoyment that it is capable of.

Confucius Saw Nancy and Essays About Nothing, p. 51

I regard the discovery of one's favorite author as the most critical event in one's intellectual development. There is such a thing as the affinity of spirits, and among the authors of ancient and modern times, one must try to find an author whose spirit is akin with his own. Only in this way can one get any real good out of reading. One has to be independent and search out his masters. Who is one's favorite author, no one can tell, probably not even the man himself. It is like love at first sight. The reader cannot be told to love this one or that one, but when he has found the author he loves, he knows it himself by a kind of instinct. We have such famous cases of discoveries of authors. Scholars seem to have lived in different ages, separated by centuries, and yet their modes of thinking and feeling were so akin

149

that their coming together across the pages of a book was like a person finding his own image. . . . It is only this kind of reading, this discovery of one's favorite author, that will do one any good at all. Like a man falling in love with his sweetheart at first sight, everything is right. She is of the right height, has the right face, the right color of hair, the right quality of voice and the right way of speaking and smiling. This author is not something that a young man need be told about by his teacher. The author is just right for him; his style, his taste, his point of view, his mode of thinking, are all right. And then the reader proceeds to devour every word and every line that the author writes, and because there is a spiritual affinity, he absorbs and readily digests everything. The author has cast a spell over him, and he is glad to be under the spell, and in time his own voice and manner and way of smiling and way of talking become like the author's own. Thus he truly steeps himself in his literary lover and derives from these books sustenance for his soul. After a few years, the spell is over and he grows a little tired of this lover and seeks for new literary lovers, and after he has had three or four lovers and completely eaten them up, he emerges as an author himself. There are many readers who never fall in love, like many young men and women who flirt around and are incapable of forming a deep attachment to a particular person. They can read any and all authors, and they never amount to anything.

The Importance of Living, pp. 380–382

In writing, the only important thing in a book is the author's personal style and feeling, as shown in his judgment and likes and dislikes.

The Importance of Living, pp. 374–375

150

Literature must, in the first place, touch the human heart, and if only its picture of life is true, it cannot do any harm.

Confucius Saw Nancy and Essays About Nothing, p. 83

One doesn't read to "improve one's mind," because when one begins to think of improving his mind, all the pleasure of reading is gone. He is the type of person who says to himself: "I must read Shakespeare, and I must read Sophocles, and I must read the entire Five Foot shelf of Dr. Eliot, so I can become an educated man." I'm sure that man will never become educated. He will force himself one evening to read Shakespeare's *Hamlet* and come away, as if from a bad dream, with no greater benefit than that he is able to say that he has "read" *Hamlet*. Anyone who reads a book with a sense of obligation does not understand the art of reading.

The Importance of Living, p. 378

. . . a letter is a soliloquy, but a letter with a postscript is a conversation. . . .

The Pleasures of a Nonconformist, p. 138

There are excuses for vice, but for ugliness, none. One who cannot produce a thing of beauty should let beauty alone.

The China Critic, January 29, 1931, p. 108

When a man is wrong, he is wrong, and there is no need for one to be impressed and overawed by a great name or by the number of books that he has read and we haven't.

The Importance of Living, p. 363

"The arts are a necessity in human life. . . . It is surprising how men have learned to live without art, feel no need for it at all, let their sensibilities atrophy as it were. Then men become coarse and vulgar."

Looking Beyond, pp. 165–166

Simplicity and sweet serenity have not been literary fashions during the last decades.

On the Wisdom of America, p. 29

Has not every writer of realistic fiction claimed that he wanted to expose something for man's spiritual uplift?

The Importance of Understanding, p. 282

The man who has not the habit of reading is imprisoned in his immediate world, in respect to time and space. His life falls into a set routine; he is limited to contact and conversation with a few friends and acquaintances, and he sees only what happens in his immediate neighborhood. From this prison there is no escape. But the moment he takes up a book, he immediately enters a different world, and if it is a good book, he is immediately put in touch with one of the best talkers of the world. This talker leads him on and carries him into a different country or a different age, or unburdens to him some of his personal regrets, or discusses with him some special line or aspect of life that the reader knows nothing about. An ancient author puts him in communion with a dead spirit of long ago, and as he reads along, he begins to imagine what that ancient author looked like and what type of person he was. Both Mencius and Ssema Ch'ien, China's greatest historian, have expressed the same idea. Now to be able to live two hours out of twelve in a different world and take one's thoughts off the claims of the immediate present is, of course, a privilege to be envied by people shut up in their bodily prison.

The Importance of Living, pp. 376–377

When one is angry, the best thing is to keep one's mouth shut, the second best thing to scratch or give your opponent a black eye, the third is to scold him by word of mouth and the fourth and most stupid thing is to scold him in writing. The pen hurts more than the tongue and the tongue hurts more than the fist. For writing always leaves a mark behind.

A History of the Press and Public Opinion in China, p. 163

A good reader turns an author inside out, like a beggar turning his coat inside out in search of fleas.

The Importance of Living, p. 388

. . . every good book is worth the reader's while when there is a real communion of the spirit, and this is possible only when he feels he is being taken into the author's confidence and the author is willing to reveal to him the innermost searchings of his heart and talk, as it were, in an unbuttoned mood, collar and tie loose, as by a friend's fireside. Nobody is ever misunderstood at a fireside; he may only be disagreed with. Agreement of opinion is the least important thing; disagreement is not only profitable, but necessary to thinking. At the fireside of a friend there is many a heated argument, after which both friends see many things not seen before. The writer who is willing to let go is sure of being understood, and only friendship which can stand occasional plain speaking is worth having.

Between Tears and Laughter, p. 1

153

No one should aim at writing immortal poetry; one should learn the writing of poems merely as a way to record a meaningful moment, a personal mood, or to help the enjoyment of Nature.

The Importance of Living, p. 285

A man's character is partly born, and so is his style. The other part is just contamination.

The Importance of Living, p. 388

I am . . . getting tired of writing editorials, which art consists in saying just so much as to catch up with popular sentiment, and not quite enough to land the writer in jail.

The Little Critic: Essays, Satires and Sketches on China (First Series: 1930–1932), p. 282

If a great writer writes a great story which is played on the stage, and the audience do not cry, then something must be wrong with the actors or the audience.

Confucius Saw Nancy and Essays About Nothing, p. 50

Art has made the modern man sex conscious. I have no doubt about it. First art and then commercial exploitation of the woman's body, down to its last curve and muscular undulation and the last painted toe-nail. I have never seen every part of a woman's body so completely exploited commercially, and find it hard to understand how American women have submitted so sweetly to this exploitation of their bodies. To an Oriental, it is hard to square this commercial exploitation of the female body with respect for women. Artists call it beauty, theater-goers call

154

it art, only producers and managers honestly call it sex appeal, and men generally have a good time.

The Importance of Living, pp. 179–180

"Store up things to say, ideas, feelings, observations of life. Pour yourself out. Then lop off later; you have to have things to lop off from. There are no rules to follow in art, the theater, the novel. You have to find yourself first and everything else follows."

Looking Beyond, p. 134

When a writer hates a person and is thinking of taking up his pen to write a bitter invective against him, but has not yet seen his good side, he should lay down the pen again, because he is not yet qualified to write a bitter invective against the person.

The Importance of Living, p. 389

It seems to me the function of literature is to make us look at life more clearly, more correctly and with a truer understanding and greater sympathy.

Confucius Saw Nancy and Essays About Nothing, p. 82

He who is afraid to use an "I" in his writing will never make a good writer.

The Importance of Living, p. 392

Creative work carries with it a form of intense love which borders on mania before it can become a success.

The Importance of Understanding, p. 294

155

I write to please no one, and may displease some, for what I say will be strictly from an individual viewpoint.

From Pagan to Christian, p. 16

There are no great mysteries about literature. There is, I believe, for some people a form of stage fright with regard to writing. Some people can get up and speak before an audience, and some can't. Some people are the best of men, but when they take pen in hand they feel lost. Writing is really only talking on paper, the difference being that one has to be more careful once it is committed to writing. It has an invisible audience, all kinds of people may read it. . . . When one has something to say and wants very much to say it, the mystery of writing is dispelled.

The Pleasures of a Nonconformist, p. 116

An experienced diplomat always coughs and lies; that is his profession. A writer should not do so. The modest cough may be very appropriate for a politician's speech, but the modest cough can be disastrous to a writer, who must, in the first place, put down exactly what he feels and thinks as an individual. The ideas and feelings must be his and his alone. A great American politician, when asked about his opinion on a big political issue, replied, "My opinion is that of the average American." That was all very well for a politician who wanted to keep his job, but it would be a damning admission for a writer if true, and extremely bad manners if false. He must say: "The moon is round, and looks scarlet to me, too. Take it or leave it, this is honestly what I think.

The Pleasures of a Nonconformist, p. 118

The only reason for writing, the only basis of authorship, is that one has something to say.

The Pleasures of a Nonconformist, p. 116

. . . it would be helpful to a beginner who aspires to be a writer first to dispel in him any over-concern with the technique of writing, and tell him to stop trifling with such superficial matters and get down to the depths of his soul, to the end of developing a genuine literary personality as the foundation of all authorship. When the foundation is properly laid and a genuine literary personality is cultivated, style follows as a natural consequence and the little points of technique will take care of themselves. It really does not matter if he is a little confused about points of rhetoric and grammar, provided he can turn out good stuff. There are always professional readers with publishing houses whose business it is to attend to the commas, semicolons, and split infinitives. On the other hand, no amount of grammatical or literary polish can make a writer if he neglects the cultivation of a literary personality. As Buffon says, "The style is the man." Style is not a method, a system or even a decoration for one's writing; it is but the total impression that the reader gets of the quality of the writer's mind, his depth or superficiality, his insight or lack of insight and other qualities like wit, humor, biting sarcasm, genial understanding, tenderness, delicacy of understanding, kindly cynicism or cynical kindliness, hardheadedness, practical common sense, and general attitude toward things. It is clear that there can be no handbook for developing a "humorous technique" or a "three-hour course in cynical kindliness," or "fifteen rules for practical common sense" and "eleven rules for delicacy of feeling."

The Importance of Living, p. 385

157

If one is too well-read, then one does not know right is right and wrong is wrong.

The Importance of Living, p. viii

It is my habit to buy cheap editions of old, obscure books and see what I can discover there. If the professors of literature knew the sources of my ideas, they would be astounded at the Philistine. But there is a greater pleasure in picking up a small pearl in an ash-can than in looking at a large one in a jeweler's window.

The Importance of Living, p. viii

The best kind of reading is bedside reading. Of course there are very important people in this world who cannot relax a moment even while they are in bed; they must think of something that will flatter their vanity, increase their body temperature and quicken their heartbeat, and make them even more important. There is also a kind of reading which is intended to excite the soul, either some ghoulish literature or a good suspense novel. This is not the kind of reading I mean. I mean reading which informs the mind and cools the understanding. True wisdom always cools and makes one see things in a better perspective. For whatever one reads, at least the position of the reader is essentially that of a spectator, and observer of life. Even when the reading matter concerns a murder, the reader has the personal comfort of knowing that he is merely an observer at the scene and not in danger of a stab at the back. That is the comfort which the Chinese describe cynically as that of watching a prairie fire across a river, knowing that you are personally safe. There is something in that fact alone. For in that position of an observer, the reader's mind can think calmly and coolly and judge human life better and more clearly and with the warmth of understanding.

158

I think the word "understanding" is a great word. It asserts the kinship of all mankind, both in its love of truth and beauty, and in its folly and its foibles. Reading of the best kind always gives that understanding of life and of oneself. That is the true purpose of reading. Reading, more than anything else, is a pure act of the mind in the privacy of one's household when the human soul holds communion with some of the wisest men of old, and in holding communion with these wise minds the soul holds communion with itself. The next morning you wake up and see some idiosyncratic behavior or doings of your friend or some member of your household and you smile more understandingly, because you have seen it before and know what some of the wisest minds think of the doings and feelings and struggles of all mankind, from time past till the present hour.

The Importance of Understanding, pp. 16–17

If a reader gets the flavor of books, he will show that flavor in his conversations, and if he has flavor in his conversations, he cannot help also having a flavor in his writing.

The Importance of Living, pp. 378–379

There are no books in this world that everybody must read, but only books that a person must read at a certain time in a given place under given circumstances and at a given period of his life. I rather think that reading, like matrimony, is determined by fate or *yinyüan.* Even if there is a certain book that every one must read, like the *Bible,* there is a time for it. When one's thoughts and experience have not reached a certain point for reading a masterpiece, the masterpiece will leave only a bad flavor on his palate.

The Importance of Living, p. 379

The modern age is an age of spiritual restlessness, both in the east and in the west. Modern art is illustrative of this restlessness.

The Pleasures of a Nonconformist, p. 297

Genuine literature is but a sense of wonder at the universe and at human life.

The Importance of Living, p. 392

Only human stupidity and certain practical needs have created something as dead and inartistic and cramping to our souls as a tall skyscraper, a factory building, or a railway track, or a street lamppost. Any of nature's trees, even the disinfected, numbered, and ugly hygienic trees that line our city boulevards, are a thousand times more beautiful than a street lamppost.

The Pleasures of a Nonconformist, pp. 254–256

No amount of money can make an uncreative mind tell a good story. A secure living made the writing by our creative minds possible, but a secure living never created anything. Money sent Charles Dickens on his American tour, but money could not produce a *David Copperfield.* Our great story-tellers, like Defoe and Fielding and Shih Nai-an and Ts'ao Hsüehch'in, wrote because they had a story to tell and because they were born story-tellers. Nature seemed to have placed Ts'ao Hsüehch'in in a fabulously luxurious home surrounding and then blasted this life all into nothingness, so that in his old age, as a bankrupt scholar and in his decrepit hut, he could recall it all like an awakened dreamer, and having relived that dream in his imagination, he felt compelled to put it down as he relived it, and we call it literature.

My Country and My People, p. 272

Simplicity of style may be all very fine, but it has the uncanny virtue of revealing emptiness of content, if one hasn't got the content. It is for this reason alone that most writers avoid simple writing.

A History of the Press and Public Opinion in China, p. 158

What, then, is the true art of reading? The simple answer is to just take up a book and read when the mood comes. To be thoroughly enjoyed, reading must be entirely spontaneous. One takes a limp volume of Lisao, or of Omar Khayyam, and goes away hand in hand with his love to read on a river bank. If there are good clouds over one's head, let them read the clouds and forget the books, or read the books and the clouds at the same time. Between times, a good pipe or a good cup of tea makes it still more perfect. Or perhaps on a snowy night, when one is sitting before the fireside, and there is a kettle singing on the hearth and a good pouch of tobacco at the side, one gathers ten or a dozen books on philosophy, economics, poetry, biography, and piles them up on the couch, and then leisurely turns over a few of them and gently lights on the one which strikes his fancy at the moment.

The Importance of Living, p. 383

The technique of writing is to literature as dogmas are to the church—the occupation with trivial things by trivial minds.

The Importance of Living, p. 386

Writing is good or bad, depending on its charm and flavor, or lack of them. For this charm there can be no rules. Charm rises from one's writing as smoke rises from a pipe-bowl, or a cloud rises from a hill-top, not knowing whither it is going. The best style is that of "sailing clouds and flowing water," like the prose of Su Tungp'o.

The Importance of Living, p. 387

A favorite author exists in the world for every man, only he hasn't taken the trouble to find him.

The Importance of Living, p. 388

There is no proper time and place for reading. When the mood for reading comes, one can read anywhere. If one knows the enjoyment of reading, he will read in school or out of school, and in spite of all schools.

The Importance of Living, p. 382

Art should be a satire and a warning against our paralyzed emotion, our devitalized thinking and our denaturalized living. It teaches us unsophistication in a sophisticated world. It should restore to us health and sanity of living and enable us to recover from the fever and delirium caused by too much mental activity. It should sharpen our senses, re-establish the connection between our reason and our human nature, and assemble the ruined parts of a dislocated life again into a whole, by restoring our original nature.

The Importance of Living, p. 142

162

The tremendous amount of time spent on newspapers I regard as not reading at all, for the average readers of papers are mainly concerned with getting reports about events and happenings without contemplative value.

The Importance of Living, p. 377

Style in cooking is like style in writing. Some people overdo it.

The Pleasures of a Nonconformist, p. 125

There are many who can write charming nonsense, but writing *charming sense* is altogether a different gift, rare as the nectar of the gods.

From Pagan to Christian, p. 130

If you command a good English style and possess a penetrating mind, you don't need a course in journalism, and if you don't, the school can't help you.

The Vigil of a Nation, p. 11

All true creative writing has an inner form of its own; the form is inherently determined by the intricacies of our thoughts, as the brook's meanderings are determined by the natural topography of the country. Any effort to adhere to conventional form can only transform the brook into a canal, the canal which carries the butcher, the baker, and the candlestick maker all swiftly and safely into the Ph. D. haven.

The Pleasures of a Nonconformist, pp. 121–122

163

The spring of creative activity must always come from the individual spirit. Literature cannot be written to a formula. Where individual spontaneity is suppressed, the creative spirit is choked at its source. A good land grows all kinds of flowers, all graceful and all different. In a marshy land, your eyes see for miles only a stretch of one color, the color of the reeds. In the spring of 1957, Chairman Mao Tsetung told the writers, "Let the hundred flowers bloom, and all schools of thought contend." The writers were encouraged officially to express themselves. Presumably, we were going to see a sudden flowering of Mao Tsetung's garden. Two months later the policy was reversed and the purge of the rightists began. Most writers who had dared to express their true feelings and opinions were sent to colonize Lanchow, Kokonor, Hainan, or some other frontier country. The beauty of a dictatorship is that a dictator does not have to explain why he condemned the free expression of opinions he had so explicitly and officially invited two months before. He did not have to—that's the beauty of it—and nobody dared to ask why. I myself would like to ask Mao Tsetung one question, "Mr. Mao, what about your garden now?"

The Pleasures of a Nonconformist, pp. 314–315

. . . a writer after all wants to be read.

The Importance of Living, p. vii

The proper use of imagination is to give beauty to the world. For as in the moral life human intelligence is used to convert the world into a place of contentment for human existence, so in the artistic life, the gift of imagination is used to cast over the commonplace workaday world a veil of beauty and make it throb with our esthetic enjoyment.

My Country and My People, pp. 98–99

A man's style is always colored by his "literary lover." He grows to be like him more and more in ways of thinking and methods of expression. That is the only way a style can be cultivated by a beginner. In later life, one finds one's own style by finding one's own self.

The Importance of Living, p. 387

生死的意義

10
ON THE
MEANING OF
LIFE AND DEATH

榊

There is no value in life except what you choose to place
upon it and no happiness in any place except what you bring to
it yourself.

On the Wisdom of America, p. 446

Belief in our mortality, the sense that we are eventually
going to crack up and be extinguished like the flame of a candle,
I say, is a gloriously fine thing. It makes us sober; it makes us a
little sad; and many of us it makes poetic. But above all, it makes
it possible for us to make up our mind and arrange to live sensibly,
truthfully and always with a sense of our own limitations. It gives
peace also, because true peace of mind comes from accepting the
worst. Psychologically, I think, it means a release of energy.

The Importance of Living, p. 158

Had there been a purpose or design in life, it should not have
been so puzzling and vague and difficult to find out.

The Importance of Living, p. 123

Our planet is a very good planet. In the first place, there is
the alternation of night and day, and morning and sunset, and a

169

cool evening following upon a hot day, and a silent and clear dawn presaging a busy morning, and there is nothing better than that. In the second place, there is the alternation of summer and winter, perfect in themselves, but made still more perfect by being gradually ushered in by spring and autumn, and there is nothing better than that. In the third place, there are the silent and dignified trees, giving us shade in summer and not shutting out the warm sunshine in winter, and there is nothing better than that. In the fourth place, there are flowers blooming and fruits ripening by rotation in the different months, and there is nothing better than that. In the fifth place, there are cloudy and misty days alternating with clear and sunny days, and there is nothing better than that. In the sixth place, there are spring showers and summer thunderstorms and the dry crisp wind of autumn and the snow of winter, and there is nothing better than that. In the seventh place, there are peacocks and parrots and skylarks and canaries singing inimitable songs, and there is nothing better than that. In the eighth place, there is the zoo, with monkeys, tigers, bears, camels, elephants, rhinoceros, crocodiles, sea lions, cows, horses, dogs, cats, foxes, squirrels, woodchucks and more variety and ingenuity than we ever thought of, and there is nothing better than that. In the ninth place, there are rainbow fish, sword fish, electric eels, whales, minnows, clams, abalones, lobsters, shrimps, turtles and more variety and ingenuity than we ever thought of, and there is nothing better than that. In the tenth place, there are magnificent redwood trees, fire-spouting volcanoes, magnificent caves, majestic peaks, undulating hills, placid lakes, winding rivers and shady banks, and there is nothing better than that. The menu is practically endless to suit individual tastes, and the only sensible thing to do is to go and partake of the feast and not complain about the monotony of life.

The Importance of Living, pp. 280–281

The fool looks to an unattainable heaven, the wise man seizes upon the immediate life. The fool looks for a future Paradise, the wise man accepts the imperfect human life on this earth. The fool waits for the next moment, the wise man eats the now. I think the man who can reveal to us the beauties and wonders of the commonplaces of life does a greater service to humanity than the poet who sends us at some rare moments into heavens of ecstatic bliss. And why? Because there are so many commonplace things around us. To discover their beauty, to appreciate their worth, to open our eyes to their human significance is truly the function of the poet and seer.

On the Wisdom of America, p. 155

The three most important things in human life are dignity of the individual, self-respect, and enough to eat.

The Pleasures of a Nonconformist, p. 24

There is nothing to be unhappy about the fact that we are, as it were, delivered upon this beautiful earth as its transient guests. Even if it were a dark dungeon, we still would have to make the best of it; it would be ungrateful of us not to do so when we have, instead of a dungeon, such a beautiful earth to live on for a good part of a century.

The Importance of Living, p. 24

. . . as we live in the human world, total abstention from activities is impossible, and so one comes to the resultant attitude of a mild passivity and indulgent quietness as the wisest mode of life.

The Wisdom of Laotse, p. 194

I have always assumed that the end of living is the true enjoyment of it.

The Importance of Living, p. 123

"Illusions are necessary to human life. They are what make life endurable. Strip the world of illusions, and we have nothing to live for. . . . Without illusions, there would be no love, no art, no religion."

Looking Beyond, p. 121

. . . as we grow older in life, our senses become gradually benumbed, our emotions become more callous to suffering and injustice and cruelty, and our vision of life is warped by too much preoccupation with cold, trivial realities.

The Importance of Living, p. 141

A wise man is content if he makes one good guess at truth in three, or if through hard thinking and striving for some general principle, as Justice Holmes did, he finally arrives at an imperfect but tolerably workable formula for living.

On the Wisdom of America, p. xii

Somehow in all countries, cranks and crackpots and schizophrenics have always believed that slovenliness is the mark of genius and that the best assurance of immortality is the refusal to dress like a gentleman. There is also a curious notion that filth and squalor imply contempt for material surroundings and therefore high spirituality, the logical con-

172

clusion of which is that heaven must reek with stinking angels.

The Gay Genius, pp. 80–81

For if there is anything unnatural in American life, it is this perpetual straining of the nervous fibre, this inability to accept quiet, the unwillingness to let the world alone for a while, the failure to insist on the right to unemployment for certain hours of the day. Pushing, ambitious young men actually are not ashamed to tell their boss that they worked on certain documents up to one o'clock on Saturday night, drove out to Cleveland and back on Sunday just for the fun of it and took a cat nap before changing and dressing for the concert that night. Such a young man evidently aims at becoming a Vice-President! Perhaps this has become natural in American life. But in no country in the world except the United States has man so wronged himself. What is natural in nature has become unnatural in man, and what is unnatural has become natural. God created all animals to play as well as to hunt for a living; only men make slaves of men. One soon forgets to listen to the wind in the pine forest, or watch the robin on the lawn. Life, even human life, was never meant that way.

What does man want in life? Does he want to change the universe? Time flows for ever; the past cannot be recaptured and the future is uncertain; only the day, the present hour, is a solid good. Perhaps the best way to thank God for the gift of living is to appreciate the present hour, to sit quietly and hear your own breathing and look out on the universe *and be content.* One can see time flow sometimes; one does not have to do something to pass the time; time can pass by itself. And there is infinite pleasure in watching the color of the day change from hour to hour and being able to say to oneself, "I have passed a perfect leisurely afternoon." Such perfect afternoons are entirely possible. There

173

is no intrusion upon one's solitude—not one telephone call, no television—one sees from the window only a child falling and bruising her leg, nothing serious, and young lovers and middle-aged couples sitting quietly on benches under trees. The world goes by. It is enough.

Or perhaps you have spent three hours in the garden, trimming branches or saving some young sprouts, or clearing the weeds and improving the garden path under a cloudless sky, and you have just come in and lit a pipe. You have been left alone, free and careless, with the passage of time, and in those hours of freedom and utter disregard for all that happens in the outside world, you have won a majesty and dignity you have seldom felt before. You have regained possession of yourself. How rarely one dares to steal such a perfect day and snatch freedom from time itself! The day passes and you are one day older. Tomorrow there is work; let's put a solid wall of sleep between the two. It is a good human life.

On the Wisdom of America, pp. 237–238

No, not your bank presidents or your builders of empires or your laborious scholars can see the truth, but your arthritic patients, your crippled, blind, and semi-invalids, your Robert Louis Stevensons and Parkmans and Prescotts and Gamaliel Bradfords, see life with a clearer and better vision.

On the Wisdom of America, p. 53

Women have a surer instinct of life than men. . . .

My Country and My People, p. 80

It is to be assumed that if man were to live this life like a poem, he would be able to look upon the sunset of his life as his happiest period, and instead of trying to postpone the much feared old age, be able actually to look forward to it, and gradually build up to it as the best and happiest period of his existence.

The Importance of Living, p. 194

Each of us falls in love . . . gets married, perhaps has a growing child, looks at the moon—and it is still the same moon. What you make of all these tremendous trifles is the burden of the wisdom of living.

On the Wisdom of America, p. 446

The span of life vouchsafed us, threescore and ten, is short enough, if the spirit gets too haughty and wants to live forever, but on the other hand, it is also long enough, if the spirit is a little humble. One can learn such a lot and enjoy such a lot in seventy years, and three generations is a long, long time to see human follies and acquire human wisdom. Anyone who is wise and has lived long enough to witness the changes of fashion and morals and politics through the rise and fall of three generations should be perfectly satisfied to rise from his seat and go away saying, "It was a good show," when the curtain falls.

The Importance of Living, pp. 23–24

Wisdom for me . . . consists in a keen sense of what we are not—that we are not gods, for instance—coupled with a willingness to face life as it is; in other words, it consists of two things, a wistfulness about living and common sense.

On the Wisdom of America, p. 3

. . . the ink that has been wasted in the discussion of free will and determinism is enough for a hippopotamus to swim in comfortably.

On the Wisdom of America, pp. 2–3

"O friends, let us take time to think about life and be unafraid, that we may see life with simplicity and clarity, without confusion and without artifices of the mind, neither looking backward, nor straining after the unattainable Beyond. Let us try to believe that life is good, and that without further waiting, the opportunity to live the good life is here, if we will it should be so. The earth is ours as we make it, society is ours as we create and improve it. Let us strive to live with our fellow men in peace and civility, that we may work fruitfully, endure nobly and live happily. Let us further take time, when our hands are freed from the toil of labor, to admire and wonder, in reverence and humility, and enjoy in beauty and in wisdom, this great spiritual universe, of which we are a part, partaking of its harmony. And when it is time for us to depart, let us leave content and grateful for having enjoyed this short, but precious gift of life."

Looking Beyond, p. 155

It is . . . a source of comfort to know that nature's instinct to live is always overpowering and manages to stage a most impressive comeback after a natural disaster.

The New York Times Magazine, November 12, 1939, p. 1

Any good practical philosophy must start out with the recognition of our having a body. It is high time that some among us made the straight admission that we are animals.

The Importance of Living, p. 24

176

Who are we? That is the first question. It is a question almost impossible to answer. But we all agree that the busy self occupied in our daily activities is not quite the real self. We are quite sure we have lost something in the mere pursuit of living. When we watch a person running about looking for something in a field, the wise man can set a puzzle for all the spectators to solve: what has that person lost? Some one thinks it is a watch; another thinks it is a diamond brooch; and others will essay other guesses. After all these guesses have failed, the wise man who really doesn't know what the person is seeking after tells the company: "I'll tell you. He has lost some breath." And no one can deny that he is right. So we often forget our true self in the pursuit of living, like a bird forgetting its own danger in pursuit of a mantis, which again forgets its own danger in pursuit of another prey. . . .

The Importance of Living, p. 96

The beauty of the human life consists in the fact that, as we review on New Year's Eve our last New Year resolutions, we find we have fulfilled a third of them, left unfulfilled another third, and can't remember what the other third was.

The Importance of Living, p. 57

A man who has to be punctually at a certain place at five o'clock has the whole afternoon from one to five ruined for him already. Every American adult is arranging his time on the pattern of the schoolboy—three o'clock for this, five o'clock for that, six-thirty for change of dress; six-fifty for entering the taxi and seven o'clock for emerging into a hotel room. It just makes life not worth living.

The Importance of Living, p. 163

177

America, we are told, is a peaceful and happy country, and it is. Why, then, don't we hear more about the joys of the common man and common woman? Somebody is scared, I do not know who. So many are nervous, and a few are wrecks. Isn't it the duty and privilege of the writers, the fresher minds, to interpret these joys for us, to remind us of them constantly—that there is this joyous common life before us? Is it not the work of the wise human mind to save for us those valuable, essential gifts of life that lie spread before us and that alone make life worth living? Isn't there somewhere always a *faith* in living as such, without thought of more discoveries and inventions? But the mind of America is directed more toward the future than the present. It is for progress and prosperity, which is a different theme altogether. It is always arriving at the next railroad station, never quite contented, never quite satisfied with where it finds itself at the present hour. That, too, is only a state of mind. A prosperous people and a happy people are two different things. My God, what the American people have lost! If they would look around at their country as it is—a peaceful and happy country, as we say, not a prosperous and progressive one—and reap the present hour, and thank God for what their country already is and not what it will be in the next decade! Even their pioneer fathers did stop and pitch a tent, and build a log cabin and raise a home somewhere, didn't they? Or were they forever moving, moving, moving?

On the Wisdom of America, pp. 152–153

There are such great souls in the world who cannot get interested in the life hereafter or in the question of immortality or in the world of spirits in general.

My Country and My People, p. 105

178

ON THE MEANING OF LIFE AND DEATH

There are moments in our life when one feels the utter futility of a daily life we are leading, and must go somewhere, or else physically or mentally collapse. This feeling is variously called the "inner urge" for independence (by overfondled children), the "divine call" (by people going abroad for adventure among heathens), "religious duty" (by the Buddhist pilgrims), or "the subliminal uprush of the nomadic instinct" (by our professors of psychology). I call it more simply "the weather."

Confucius Saw Nancy and Essays About Nothing, p. 242

. . . if life is worth anything, it is that it teaches a lesson of kindliness.

My Country and My People, p. 52

For the ideal philosopher is one who understands the charm of women without being coarse, who loves life heartily but loves it with restraint, and who sees the unreality of the successes and failures of the active world, and stands somewhat aloof and detached, without being hostile to it.

The Importance of Living, p. 116

The scientist knocks and the door refuses to open; at the moment he is about to discover the secret of life, life shuts up completely.

The Wisdom of Laotse, p. 17

Only by alternating between the absolutely erect working posture of office hours and the posture of stretching ourselves on

179

a sofa after a hard day's work can we achieve that highest wisdom of living.

The Importance of Living, p. 210

Each one has found life as he makes it.

On the Wisdom of America, p. 448

A younger civilization may be keen on making progress, but an old civilization, having seen naturally a great deal of life, is keen only on living.

My Country and My People, p. 325

. . . life is full of after-thoughts and hesitations and regrets for indiscretions and sudden comedowns from philosophic heights as well as sudden flashes of heroic resolutions.

The Little Critic: Essays, Satires and Sketches on China (Second Series: 1933–1935), p. 166

It is that unoccupied space which makes a room habitable, as it is our leisure hours which make life endurable.

The Importance of Living, p. 151

"Lots of people who have never entered the door of Tiffany's in this earthly life hope to do so in the next."

Looking Beyond, p. 129

Our preoccupation with immortality has something pathological about it.

The Importance of Living, p. 399

. . . many men today are quite content to be just dead when they die.

The Importance of Living, p. 398

If some people can be kept good by the fear of hell, others can be kept good by the fear of a bad name after death.

A History of the Press and Public Opinion in China, p. 25

After all, we have to get on in this life, and so we must bring philosophy down from heaven to earth.

The Importance of Living, p. 115

Life or existence does not have to go down on its knees and beg logic to prove that it exists or that it is there.

The Importance of Living, p. 420

Life is so relative that we would not dare to pass dogmatic judgments.

On the Wisdom of America, p. 353

I have no sympathy for those who believe that they have a reserved seat in heaven.

From Pagan to Christian, p. 15

Hell decreases its importance as the FBI increases its efficiency.

On the Wisdom of America, p. 341

That men should die is hard enough for the mothers of men; that they should die in vain is heartbreaking.

Between Tears and Laughter, p. 54

No one can say that a life with childhood, manhood and old age is not a beautiful arrangement; the day has its morning, noon and sunset, and the year has its seasons, and it is good that it is so. There is no good or bad in life, except what is good according to its own season. And if we take this biological view of life and try to live according to the seasons, no one but a conceited fool or an impossible idealist can deny that human life can be lived like a poem.

The Importance of Living, pp. 31–32

Into this question of what should be the purpose of human life, every man projects his own conceptions and his own scale of values. It is for this reason that we quarrel over the question, because our scales of values differ from one another. For myself, I am content to be less philosophical and more practical. I should not presume that there must be necessarily a purpose, a meaning of human existence. As Walt Whitman says, "I am sufficient as I am." It is sufficient that I live—and am probably going to live for another few decades —and that human life exists. Viewed that way, the problem becomes amazingly simple and admits of no two answers. What can be the end of human life except the enjoyment of it?

The Importance of Living, p. 124

Good, bad, or indifferent, big or small, our influences continue; the things we do and the words we say live after us in the huge stream of life, which goes on forever. Some send out longer waves, and some make only slight ripples on their neighbors or their orphans and affect them, their lives and their beliefs, somehow. But even the slightest ripple in the ocean of life has some effect on its neighboring atoms. And so we go on punishing and rewarding those who live after us. As for being punished or rewarded in some future life, I am totally uninterested.

On the Wisdom of America, pp. 89–90

If the question is asked, "What are you doing in this life?" the fisherman can answer it more easily and quickly than the rest. "I am enjoying life—this gift of living." "How rarely in life does one laugh aloud!" says the Chinese poet. Meanwhile, a startled bird's cry from the woods, a muffled groan of some unknown animal, or a sudden plop in the water reaches our ears, and we are taken out of our own preoccupations and realize that life is spread before us as it was from the beginning, is now and ever shall be. Submerged in our daily activities, we have cut ourselves entirely from nature; suddenly we are puzzled as to the true meaning and purpose of this life. We retake possession of our true selves.

The Pleasures of a Nonconformist, p. 20

If a chicken has been killed, and it is not cooked properly, that chicken has died in vain.

The Pleasures of a Nonconformist, p. 124

183

True enough, we all have obligations and duties toward our fellow men. But it does seem curious enough that in modern, neurotic society, men's energies are consumed in making a living, and rarely in living itself. It takes a lot of courage for a man to declare, with clarity and simplicity, that the purpose of life is to enjoy it.

The Pleasures of a Nonconformist, pp. 20–21

Life is a huge farce, and we human beings are mere puppets in it. The man who takes life too seriously, who obeys library reading-room rules too honestly, who actually keeps off the lawn because merely a signboard says so, always makes a fool of himself and is usually subjected to laughter from his older colleagues, and since laughter is contagious, very soon he becomes a humorist, too.

My Country and My People, p. 69

That the end of living is just living itself is so obvious that we never thought of it, and in times of peace we even question it. Moralists, for example, seem to despise the act of lying in bed, and theologians used to think that to be uncomfortable was to be virtuous. But in the soldier at the front the conviction must sooner or later grow that lying in bed is one of the supreme gifts of civilization and that to sleep with one's boots off is an incomparably truer form of living than sleeping with one's boots on.

The New York Times Magazine, November 12, 1939, p. 16

. . . in food, as in death, we feel the essential brotherhood of mankind.

The Importance of Living, p. 46

184

Change means chaos, but it also means life.

The New York Times Magazine, November 22, 1936, p. 11

For life, after all the vain struggle for money and glory, boils down to a few things, which are mainly physical, like good food, a good home, a peaceful heart without worry and a good bowl of hot congee on a cold morning. All the rest is vanity of vanities.

The Little Critic: Essays, Satires and Sketches on China (Second Series: 1933–1935), p. 16

As we know more and more we seem to understand less and less. My point is that as science knows more and more, we wonder more and more also, as any good scientist can tell you. Science, and this covers all branches of science, can answer the question "How?" but can never answer the ultimate question "Why?"

The Pleasures of a Nonconformist, p. 85

. . . the world is not a syllogism or an argument, it is a being; the universe does not talk, it lives; it does not argue, it merely gets there.

The Importance of Living, p. 421

. . . the great end of any man's existence is to find his place in life—and that is the secret of contentment. Life is again like the picture of a man who finds himself in an overcrowded railroad car. If he has found his place in that crowded car, he is happy and contented; if not, he isn't. There are busybodies who neglect to do that, but rather think it to be their duty to take that carload

185

of people in hand and reform the passengers—to object to a neighbor's protruding legs, to tell him to put his coat in some other place, to demand the opening or shutting of windows as he feels hot or cold, and to hush some one behind who perhaps talks too loud, his "hushing" being louder than the talking. He does not know that order will establish itself in five minutes by every man finding a place for himself, and that if he is not to be a restless nervous wreck at the end of the journey his first duty is to find his own place in that temporary community.... The secret of contentment is the discovery by every man of his own powers and limitations, finding satisfaction in a line of activity which he can do well, plus the wisdom to know that his place, no matter how important or successful he is, never counts very much in the universe. A man may very well be so successful in carving a name for himself in his field that he begins to imagine himself indispensable or omnipotent. He is eaten up by some secret ambition, and then goodby to all contentment. Sometimes it is more important to discover what one cannot do, than what one can do. So much restlessness is due to the fact that a man does not know what he wants, or he wants too many things, or perhaps he wants to be somebody else, to be anybody except himself. The courage of being one's genuine self, of standing alone and of not wanting to be somebody else!

On the Wisdom of America, pp. 225–226

The restitution of the simple values of life is the first task of modern man's intelligence.

The Pleasures of a Nonconformist, p. 21

... if this earthly existence is all we have, we must try the harder to enjoy it while it lasts. A vague hope of immortality

186

detracts from our wholehearted enjoyment of this earthly existence.

The Importance of Living, p. 156

We have lost the gift of seeing life steadily and seeing life whole.

My Country and My People, p. 280

. . . how fortunate is man that he is born between the real earth and the unreal heaven!

The Importance of Living, p. 24

. . . there is a danger that our solid citizens may become too solid, and then goodbye to all thinking, to all fanciful imaginings, and glimpses of truth. Breathes there a soul so dead that he never wants to be something more than a good father or a good child? After all debts are paid and one's children are sent to the best school in town does one never ask, Who am I and what have I become? Is one truly satisfied, or does somewhere from the unknown depths of man a doubt arise? I am the doubter and the doubt. Who am I? How did the universe begin? What lies beyond? Surely, despite that solid good sense of duty, one has sometimes a lurking desire to explore the beyond, to take a daring leap into the dark void and ask a question or two of God Himself.

From Pagan to Christian, pp. 108–109

Life . . . is really a dream, and we human beings are like travelers floating down the eternal river of time, embarking at a certain point and disembarking again at another point in order to make room for others waiting below the river to come aboard. Half of the poetry of life would be gone, if we did not feel that

187

life was either a dream, or a voyage with transient travelers, or merely a stage in which the actors seldom realized that they were playing their parts.

The Importance of Living, p. 41

Can there be a universal human ideal? The answer is probably no. Every man must find his own philosophy. Every man has, in fact, his own philosophy, his attitude toward life.

On the Wisdom of America, pp. 447–448

I suspect that all democracy, all poetry, and all philosophy start out from this God-given fact that all of us, princes and paupers alike, are limited to a body of five or six feet and live a life of fifty or sixty years. On the whole, the arrangement is quite handy. We are neither too long nor too short. At least I am quite satisfied with five feet four. And fifty or sixty years seems to me such an awfully long time; it is, in fact, a matter of two or three generations. It is so arranged that when we are born, we see certain old grandfathers, who die in the course of time, and when we become grandfathers ourselves, we see other tiny tots being born. That seems to make it just perfect.

The Importance of Living, p. 38

We are confronted here with a strange fact of the universe, the pure, blessed desire to do good, to love and to help others as a final fact without explanation. This is the wonder of the universe, that man strives toward the good, and feels compelled inwardly to perfect himself, almost as the salmon instinctively goes upstream to spawn.

From Pagan to Christian, p. 196

188

We live in a world without belief, a world of moral cynicism, of collapse of valid human ideals. And all of us are paying for that collapse of human ideals.

From Pagan to Christian, p. 226

He who perceives death perceives a sense of the human comedy, and quickly becomes a poet.

The Importance of Living, pp. 39–40

神及宗教

11
ON GOD
AND
RELIGION

To thank God for a good wind is sheer impudence, and selfishness also, for it implies that God does not love the people sailing south when HE, the important individual, is sailing north.

The Importance of Living, p. 397

One need not argue whether God created the stars for man to look at. We shall never know. But if it is good to look at the stars, look at them.

On the Wisdom of America, p. 447

I have a feeling that God always works through the mob. The mob, after all, has a certain Divine Right. My inspiration does not necessarily come from the Chinese *Book of History,* which says, "God listens through the ears of the people and speaks through the mouth of the people." It comes from an intuitive insight and from my observation of history. When the mob is resentful, it is God who is resentful. When the mob is enraged, be sure God is enraged. When the mob is violent and uses the guillotine, it is God who thinks it is time to be violent and invent the guillotine. When the mob hesitates, it is God who hesitates. And when the mob goes back to its homes to pursue the daily business of life, it is God who is happy.

193

Therefore when the public sentiment condemns a public policy, it is God who condemns it.

Between Tears and Laughter, pp. 98–99

It is easier to destroy a pet notion of "Heaven" and "Hell" than to destroy the notion of God.

The Importance of Living, p. 396

All I know is that if God loves me only half as much as my mother does, he will not send me to Hell.

The Importance of Living, p. 407

Beware of the man who always finds God on his side.

Between Tears and Laughter, p. 35

Abraham Lincoln said that God must love the common people because He made so many of them. That was a clever, religious statement, by which I mean a statement which is true not because it is true but because we already choose to believe it anyway. Philosophically, of course, it does not have a leg to stand on. God made many more fish in the Pacific Ocean than men on the American continent. He also made many more flies and ants, not to speak of bacteria. I haven't got statistics about bacteria, and nobody else has, but of course the figures are astronomical. So God must love bacteria more than man. But even if He does, we choose not to believe it. God made some of them so they can even survive subzero temperature and boiling water. A philosophical proof of the common man thesis evidently cannot be maintained. The establishment of the philosophical proof is difficult, because the parts never measure up to the whole and the philosophers who

194

express their love and trust in their fellow men quite often go to the bank or the market or the subway and are sadly disillusioned.

On the Wisdom of America, p. 178

Faith is belief in something on inadequate evidence.

The Pleasures of a Nonconformist, p. 90

Tolerance is a rare virtue among followers of religions.

From Pagan to Christian, p. 16

Popular imagination always created the necessary gods if the philosophers refused to do so.

From Pagan to Christian, p. 147

. . . religion is essentially a reverence for life.

The Importance of Understanding, p. 421

It is true that there are more things which God can do than are dreamed of in man's religion, but it is equally true that much in religion is attributed to God that God never dreamed of doing.

From Pagan to Christian, p. 185

I have come by religion the hard way, and I think this is the only way, and do not think there is any other way to give it the necessary validity. For religion is, first and last, an individual facing up to the astounding heavens, a matter between him and God. It is a matter of individual growth *from within*, and cannot be "given" by anybody. For religion is a flower which is best grown in a field, and the pot-grown or hot-house variety is apt to be pale-colored, as well as fragile and friable.

From Pagan to Christian, p. 14

Let religion respectfully keep its mouth shut when teachers of biology are talking, and it will seem infinitely less silly and gain immeasurably in the respect of mankind.

The Importance of Living, p. 397

If religion means otherworldliness, I reject it. If religion means that we must run away from this present, sentient life and "escape" from it as fast as possible, like a rat abandoning a sinking ship, I am against it. One ought to, I think, with Chinese common sense, come to live with the world and make terms with it, bravely, in the sense of the acceptance of the grace of living as the Shan believers do. And I feel strongly that so long as religion, *any* religion, clings to an otherworldliness, this tendency to deny and escape from this sentient life which God has given us so abundantly, we will, by doing so, by just so much prevent religion, *any* religion, from being in touch with the modern man's consciousness. We shall be in a true sense ungrateful children of God, not even worthy cousins of the Shan believers.

From Pagan to Christian, p. 176

Our lives are not in the lap of the gods, but in the lap of our cooks.

The Importance of Living, p. 248

196

. . . I am so profoundly religious by nature that "religions" often make me furious.

The Nation, May 6, 1939, p. 526

The basis of all religions is the cold fact of human mortality.

On the Wisdom of America, p. 85

The thought has been constantly on my mind to find a religion that is acceptable to a scientist. For this is the central problem of the age.

The Wisdom of Laotse, p. 15

The eternal mystery! Who would not like to rend the curtain hiding it? Who would not like to know the hand of God, to see with all-comprehending wisdom the careful, cunning workmanship of the Great Author of this greatest mystery story and cease from guessing or suspecting everyone present of having committed countless murders in the universe since existence began? This tremendous, monstrous whodunit has never been solved.

On the Wisdom of America, p. 21

Every person must work out his own views of religion, and if he is sincere, God will not blame him, however it turns out. Every man's religious experience is valid for himself, for . . . it is not something that can be argued about.

The Importance of Living, p. 400

The sight of a Christian who actually practices Christian kindness and concern for individuals always tended to bring me

197

closer to the Christian Church. . . . Christians breed Christians, but Christian theology does not.

From Pagan to Christian, pp. 233–234

We human creatures who individually are less than a billionth part of the earth's crust, which is less than a billionth part of the great universe, presume to know God!

The Importance of Living, p. 396

We should be able just to look at each other and love each other without being reminded of a third party in heaven.

The Importance of Living, p. 408

Modern discoveries about the atom and subatomic particles cannot but change a man's religion or view of life, whatever it may be. It is altogether too upsetting.

From Pagan to Christian, p. 210

"Why should we try to place God exactly where he is? We wish to codify God and never ask whether God wishes to be codified by us."

Looking Beyond, p. 337

You can never prove the existence of God in the laboratory sense of scientific proof; nor can you disprove it. You can never prove immortality. Objectively, from a study of nature, you can never prove that God is Love. Neither can love itself ever be controlled by reason. "The heart has its reasons of which Reason cannot know," says the great Pascal. The universe has secrets

198

which can be apprehended only by a higher intelligence, the gift of direct, immediate insight.

The Pleasures of a Nonconformist, p. 46

If the kingdom of God is within you, how can depravity be "total"? How difficult it is for this truth to penetrate theological minds!

From Pagan to Christian, p. 175

Science tells men to inquire, the church tells men to stop inquiring. But what is the worth of the freedom of belief if we haven't the freedom to inquire?

On the Wisdom of America, p. 344

A pagan always believes in God, but is afraid of saying so for fear of being misunderstood.

From Pagan to Christian, pp. 186–187

Is faith to be based on knowledge, or does faith only begin where knowledge ends?

The Importance of Living, p. 398

"Creeds were formed when the Christian fathers began to argue."

Looking Beyond, p. 168

Religious people today support the church not because they believe or ever think much about its dogmas, but rather because they tolerate them and are willing to leave them alone.

On the Wisdom of America, p. 343

. . . one can truly understand any foreign creed or religion or country only when one enters to live in spirit in that new world.

The Importance of Living, p. 138

"No, you don't get away from idols in any human society. We must either make gods like men, or make gods of men. The public must have something to worship. The worst thing is to have nothing to worship—to gaze perhaps at the steam radiator which you put your tired foot on. That is where the modern economic man has come to, why he is so sad, so uprooted, so scientific and so worried."

Looking Beyond, p. 130

Such religion as there can be in modern life, every individual will have to salvage from the churches for himself.

The Importance of Living, p. 397

. . . the pagan lives in this world like an orphan, without the benefit of that consoling feeling that there is always some one in heaven who cares and who will, when that spiritual relationship called prayer is established, attend to his private personal welfare. It is no doubt a less cheery world; but there is the benefit and dignity of being an orphan who by necessity has learned to be independent, to take care of himself, and to be more mature, as all orphans are.

The Importance of Living, p. 402

Isn't the peculiarity of Christ that He made one feel a better and worthier person instead of a sinner in His Presence?

From Pagan to Christian, p. 238

Everybody believes in something, nobody can believe in nothing.

The Pleasures of a Nonconformist, p. 97

. . . I believe that the only kind of religious belief left for the modern man is a kind of mysticism in the broadest sense of the word, such as was preached by Laotse. Broadly speaking, it consists in reverence and respect for the moral order of the universe, philosophic resignation to the moral order, and the effort to live in harmony with this moral order.

The Nation, May 6, 1939, p. 528

For no man lives alone in this world, and all religions have to cope with the problem of the loneliness of the human soul. That the human soul is individual and lonely is the reason for all religions and for all organizations such as clubs, societies, the church, and the state.

From Pagan to Christian, pp. 97–98

Religion cannot be, and should not be, anything except an inspiration and a living emotion.

My Country and My People, p. 242

201

That is America's social difficulty, the right of every man to believe in God in his own way and the social duty not to talk about it to others. The correct thing in good company is, talk about God, but if you have anything to say, don't say it.

On the Wisdom of America, p. 310

It has always seemed to me that wherever the spirit of man lives, religion comes to life again. Whenever the spirit of man dies, religion also decays.

The Importance of Understanding, p. 206

Before the cock crows thrice we deny Truth again and again.

On the Wisdom of America, p. xiv

. . . you can't make a man a Christian unless you first make him believe he is a sinner.

The Importance of Living, p. 17

There are form and content in any religion, and religion always expresses itself through form. In the case of Christianity, the content was given by Jesus in all its plenitude, but the form was added by man.

From Pagan to Christian, pp. 239–240

. . . poetry is but truth colored with emotion, music is sentiment without words, and religion is but wisdom expressed in fancy.

The Importance of Living, p. 140

From the beginning of history, man has always cried for some kind of faith, something to believe in.

The Pleasures of a Nonconformist, p. 82

12
ON
HUMAN
ADJUSTMENTS

This is the dilemma of the modern man. Human nature cannot change. It will not change. This is hardly a comforting thought.

The Pleasures of a Nonconformist, p. 31

I feel sure that the child gets his first initiation into the sorrows of this life when his mother forbids him to smack his lips.

The Importance of Living, p. 47

All Æsop's Fables are libels on the animal kingdom, and would not get a chance of being understood by the animals if they could read them. When a fox fails to reach a hanging bunch of grapes, he just gets away: he is not such a bad sport as to call them "sour grapes." No animal except man can descend to such a low level.

The Little Critic: Essays, Satires and Sketches on China (Second Series: 1933–1935), p. 144

I do not know whether to understand is to forgive, but at least, let us try to understand.

The Secret Name, p. 13

A layman is a man who suggests that a thing can be done, and an expert is one who knows exactly how a thing can't be done.

Between Tears and Laughter, p. 96

Is it not our weakness that makes our strength?

The Importance of Understanding, p. 118

I am told that committees are formed to make decisions by the vote of the majority. It is nothing of the kind. It is a fine form of bureaucratic system invented so that nobody need make any decision at all.

The Pleasures of a Nonconformist, p. 32

The idea of women trying to ape men in their manners is in itself a sign of women's bondage. Let women be proud of their own sex, for only in the fulfilment of their sex and its grave responsibilities will they be truly great.

My Country and My People, p. 171

. . . no business man who does not retire at fifty, if he can, is in my eyes a philosopher.

The Importance of Living, p. 13

Man makes the law, and man is always able to beat it. . . .

Looking Beyond, p. 146

I am willing to allow that smoking is a moral weakness, but on the other hand, we must beware of the man without weak-

208

nesses. He is not to be trusted. He is apt to be always sober and he cannot make a single mistake. His habits are likely to be regular, his existence more mechanical and his head always maintains its supremacy over his heart.

The Importance of Living, p. 231

We accept what we are used to and never think about it.

The Pleasures of a Nonconformist, p. 194

. . . a man who has qualms of conscience cannot have a sense of humor at the same time.

The Little Critic: Essays, Satires and Sketches on China (First Series: 1930–1932), p. 91

By being consistent, we miss many of the best things in life.

The Pleasures of a Nonconformist, p. 56

Human ingenuity is such that you can get anything you want, give it any name you want, fool the people enough for a time to make them believe that they have got what really they haven't, and fool other people enough to desire what those people haven't got but the outsiders think that they have, by juggling with words.

On the Wisdom of America, p. 177

. . . the downfall of man and the coquetry of woman began with a fig-leaf.

Confucius Saw Nancy and Essays About Nothing, p. 91

209

Man has undoubtedly been unfair to woman, yet it is interesting to see how sometimes woman has her revenge.

My Country and My People, p. 144

"A young man is capable of doing anything when a pretty girl is around."

Looking Beyond, p. 278

. . . when a man is at peace with himself, he cannot understand the youthful enthusiasm for progress and reform. It is the old culture of an old people who know life for what it is worth and do not strive for the unattainable.

My Country and My People, p. 44

Nothing succeeds in this world without taking the trouble.

The Pleasures of a Nonconformist, p. 116

Mere sluggishness of mind or body does not make one a philosopher.

From Pagan to Christian, p. 111

All men are neurotic one way or another.

From Pagan to Christian, p. 175

The strain of keeping up sex appeal necessarily falls upon the nerves of women and not of men. It is also unfair, for by placing

210

a premium upon beauty and youth, middle-aged women are confronted with the hopeless task of fighting their gray hair and time's course. A Chinese poet has already warned us that the fountain of youth is a hoax, that no man can yet "tie a string to the sun" and hold back its course. Middle-aged woman's effort to keep up sex appeal thus becomes an arduous race with the years, which is quite senseless. Only humor can save the situation. If there is no use carrying on a hopeless fight against old age and white hair, why then not call the white hair beautiful?

The Importance of Living, p. 181

. . . it is undeniable that the older we grow, the more shameless we become.

My Country and My People, p. 54

"Always admire the good in others, and forget not sometimes to admire the good in yourself."

Looking Beyond, p. 150

. . . no one can go about conquering the world if he has doubts about himself.

The Importance of Living, p. 62

"All men think of women better than women think of themselves."

Looking Beyond, p. 121

211

I have never pretended to like the people who dislike me. I have never been suave and polished and dishonest.

The Little Critic: Essays, Satires and Sketches on China (Second Series: 1933–1935), p. 192

Is it not sufficient that the old people *are* something? Is it necessary that they must be forever *doing* something? The loss of the capacity for loafing is bad enough in men of middle age, but the same loss in old age is a crime committed against human nature.

The Importance of Living, p. 164

The true father of all juvenile delinquency is the "social scientist." Spank the social "scientist" on the bottom, and juvenile delinquents will disappear.

The Pleasures of a Nonconformist, p. 93

. . . it is in one's childhood that a man's habits are formed and his general attitude toward his fellow men is established. He is either rebellious and inconsiderate of others and has no regard for good form in social conduct, or he has learned to consider others and to give respect and affection to those to whom respect and affection are due.

From Pagan to Christian, p. 100

Both men and women love to exaggerate the differences.

On the Wisdom of America, p. 68

How can any one deny that parents who have toiled for their children in their youth, have lost many a good night's sleep when they were ill, have washed their diapers long before they could talk and have spent about a quarter of a century bringing them up and fitting them for life, have the right to be fed by them and loved and respected when they are old?

The Importance of Living, p. 199

A mistake is something which it is the privilege of the great men to commit and of the small men of this earth to point out after they are dead.

Between Tears and Laughter, p. 9

All forgiveness is illogical, yet we must fear a man who never forgives.

The Pleasures of a Nonconformist, p. 43

In the office, women talk with civility; outside the office, they talk with authority.

The Importance of Living, p. 178

Affairs are sometimes too complicated to be clarified even by a personal discussion.

The Gay Genius, p. 291

No one should be a crass materialist or a starry-eyed idealist. Both are dangers to mankind.

On the Wisdom of America, p. 105

213

One argues because one is confused. The man who knows does not argue; the man who argues does not know.

The Pleasures of a Nonconformist, p. 44

. . . to err is bestial, but to laugh at our errors is human.

Asia, October, 1946, p. 455

Man naturally becomes conservative when he realizes he has got something that works and therefore something that is true.

My Country and My People, p. 72–73

No modern man can still believe with Shakespeare that "Frailty, thy name is woman." Shakespeare disproved this himself with his Cleopatra, and with King Lear's daughters.

My Country and My People, p. 145

Most Americans haven't got the good sense to take a chicken drumstick in their hand and chew it clean, but continue to pretend to play at it with a knife and fork, feeling utterly miserable and afraid to say a thing about it. This is criminal when the chicken is really good.

The Importance of Living, p. 47

I was foolish enough once to stop smoking for three weeks, but at the end of that period, in my case, my conscience irresistibly urged me on to the right road again.

The Little Critic: Essays, Satires and Sketches on China (First Series: 1930–1932), p. 275

"The proper study of woman is man."

Looking Beyond, p. 105

Somehow intellectual women have to insist that they have the normal emotions of a woman.

Looking Beyond, p. 19

The courage to be one's own natural self is quite a rare thing.

The Importance of Living, p. 104

Any true philosopher ought to be ashamed of himself when he sees a child, or even a lion cub in a cage. How perfectly nature has fashioned him with his paws, his muscles, his beautiful coat of fur, his pricking ears, his bright round eyes, his agility and his sense of fun!

The Importance of Living, p. 143

The folly that men do is enough to make the angels weep.

The Secret Name, p. 10

. . . men determine events, events do not determine men.

From Pagan to Christian, p. 78

A banker may be the gentlest of fathers and the kindest of friends, but in the execution of his professional duties, he would be a silly fool if he were to grow sentimental over driving a competitor out of business.

The Little Critic: Essays, Satires and Sketches on China (Second Series: 1933–1935), p. 184

Nothing so unites two enemies as the knowledge that they have been the common victim of a third mischievous party.

Between Tears and Laughter, pp. 119–120

An average Chinese child knows what the European gray-haired statesmen do not know, that by fighting one gets killed or maimed, whether it be an individual or a nation.

My Country and My People, p. 59

There are so few things one can be sure about that it does one good to see a man who can be so sure of himself.

With Love and Irony, p. 14

Somehow Dr. Johnson's gout is exciting to us even today, while Milton's blindness is not.

The Gay Genius, p. 3

All of us have the desire to get out of an old rut, and all of us wish to be something else, and all of us dream.

The Importance of Living, p. 73

When a man says, "I don't know why I am doing this," you may be sure that he is acting on his best impulse, against all reason. It proves that he is a good man.

The Pleasures of a Nonconformist, p. 43

I think that human feet as God made them for walking are perfect. There can be no improvement upon them, and wearing shoes is a form of human degeneracy.

From Pagan to Christian, p. 42

No one is objective; he who thinks he is only deceives himself.

On the Wisdom of America, p. 446

As for the sixth sense, I see as many women lose at the roulette table as men, the sixth sense being the inability to tell clearly why you want to do a thing when you do it.

On the Wisdom of America, p. 68

"No man should be fairly asked to imitate the gods. Be ye as perfect. . . . We are *not* gods. Suppose you are not a Galli-Curci, or a Paderewski, and you strive to be such a one, you will kill yourself in the attempt, won't you? You will hate yourself, your audience, your critics, and society in general. It creates a psychic tension, a feeling of inadequacy and guilt, that you are not what you should be. You become neurotic so long as the conflict, the disparity between the ideal and the real, cannot be resolved, and you generate certain destructive tendencies, such as love for

217

war-making and the desire to annihilate somebody. You've got to shift the blame somewhere."

Looking Beyond, p. 149

With a man who simply chooses to believe, arguments are a pure waste.

Confucius Saw Nancy and Essays About Nothing, p. 239

When we call a man great, we mean by it our inability to understand him.

The Little Critic: Essays, Satires and Sketches on China (First Series: 1930–1932), p. 21

Half of the world spends its time doing things, and half the world spends its time making others do things for them, or making it impossible for others to do anything.

The Importance of Living, pp. 50–51

I am not against any particular dogma, but rather against a more basic evil, the spirit of dogmatism itself.

On the Wisdom of America, p. 338

Successful business men and gold-diggers want the same thing, money, and they ought to respect each other for his or her clearmindedness.

My Country and My People, p. 143

The world is therefore pretty much like an *à la carte* restaurant where everybody thinks the food the next table has ordered is so much more inviting and delicious than his own.

The Importance of Living, p. 74

Everyone wants to be somebody so long as that somebody is not himself.

The Importance of Living, p. 74

Nothing shows more conclusively a small mind than a little government bureaucrat suffering from illusions of his own grandeur, or a social upstart displaying her jewels, or a half-baked writer imagining himself to belong to the company of the immortals and immediately becoming a less simple and less natural human being.

The Importance of Living, p. 105

. . . hatred is an expression of incompetence. . . .

The Gay Genius, p. ix

We need a certain kindness and generosity to ourselves before we learn kindness and generosity to others.

The Importance of Living, p. 249

"Anything the people believe in, they straightway make a god of it."

Looking Beyond, p. 121

219

"Do not try to appear better than you are, nor worse than is really necessary."

Looking Beyond, p. 150

I think the only kind of progress which everybody will agree on and want is that everybody shall have more money to spend.

The Pleasures of a Nonconformist, p. 29

The desire for one hundred per cent efficiency seems almost obscene.

The Importance of Living, p. 162

No matter how important or unimportant we are, how good or wicked or mediocre, we cannot hope to escape the effect our individual lives have upon others. Even the sight of mediocrity produces an effect upon one's students or neighbors.

On the Wisdom of America, p. 89

. . . I always come home a mental wreck from cocktail parties, at which one attains the maximum physical movement with the minimum mental activity. A cocktail party is a place where you talk with a person you do not know about a subject you have no interest in.

With Love and Irony, p. 28

The world today is divided into smokers and non-smokers. It is true that the smokers cause some nuisance to the non-